# Glorious Christmas Crafts

# Glorious Christmas Crafts

*Celebrate the Holidays with More Than 120 Festive Projects to Make*

Diane LaRose-Weaver
& Dawn Cusick

 **A Sterling/Lark Book**
Sterling Publishing Co., Inc.    New York

To my husband Dick, who is ever ready to help and liberal with his
praise, encouragement, and love — Diane

Photography: Evan Bracken, Light Reflections, Hendersonville, NC
Art Director: Diane LaRose-Weaver
Production: Elaine Thompson

**Library of Congress CIP Data Available**

10 9 8 7 6 5 4 3 2 1

**A Sterling/Lark Book**

First paperback edition published in 1993 by
Sterling Publishing Company, Inc.
387 Park Avenue South, New York, N.Y. 10016

Produced by Altamont Press, Inc.
50 College Street, Asheville, NC 28801

Originally published in hardcover
as *A Fireside Christmas*
© 1992, Altamont Press

Distributed in Canada by Sterling Publishing
℅ Canadian Manda Group, P.O. Box 920, Station U
Toronto, Ontario, Canada M8Z 5P9
Distributed in Great Britain and Europe by Cassell PLC
Villiers House, 41/47 Strand, London WC2N 5JE, England
Distributed in Australia by Capricorn Link Ltd.
P.O. Box 665, Lane Cove, NSW 2066

Every effort has been made to ensure that all the information in this book
is accurate. However, due to differing conditions, tools, and individual
skills, the publisher cannot be responsible for any injuries, losses, or other
damages which may result from the use of the information in this book.

Printed and bound in Hong Kong

Sterling ISBN 0-8069-8379-5

# CONTENTS

• • • • • • • • • • •

# CONTRIBUTING DESIGNERS

●●●●●●●●●●●

**Maureen Donahue**
(pages 76, 77, 85, 92-left, and 94) lives in Santa Clara, California, where she runs her graphic design company, Cha Cha Graphics. Maureen relaxes from the stresses of work by creating miniatures.

**Dot McMullen**
(pages 93-bottom, 98-bottom, and 103-105) manages a fabric store in Waynesville, North Carolina, and enjoys all varieties of fabric crafts.

**Diane Weaver**
(pages 12-18, 23-29, 32-35, 38, 45, 48, 52, 56, 57, 58, 72, 74, 75, 76, 78-83, 86, 87-top, 88-bottom, 93-bottom, 116-119, 122-center, 126, 127, and 132-137) is a painter at heart who lives and works at her and husband Dick's herb farm, Gourmet Gardens, in Weaverville, North Carolina.

**Cynthia Gillooly**
(pages 18-bottom, 19-bottom, 22, 23-left, and 87-bottom ) owns and operates The Golden Cricket in Asheville, North Carolina, and specializes in innovate, natural designs.

**Liz and Pete Sullivan**
(pages 39, 43, 89-bottom, 95, 100-top left, and 132-bottom) own an antique restoration and reproduction shop in the mountains of North Carolina.

**Also thanks to . . .**
Carolyn Alexander (page 128), Paula Barnes (pages 90 and 91), Carol Burnette from The Folk Art Sampler (pages 89-top and 99), Judy Councill (page 42-right), Charlie Covington (page 136), Jo Lydia Craven (page 45-ornaments), Dawn Cusick (page 72-top and 73), Joyce Cusick (page 49), Constance Daly (page 124-center), Eula Haynes (page 72), Candy Hinman (pages 67-bottom left, 68, and 69), Earlene Hoffman (pages 93-top and 98-top), Jim Hoffman (page 77-center bottom), Tina Kelley (pages 72, 116, 126-top, and 127-top), Carol Koronus (pages 59 and 115), Janie Markley (pages 112 and 113),

**Suzanne Koppi**
(pages 36, 37, 103-bottom, 107-109, 122-stars, 130, and 131) is a special education teacher in Black Mountain, North Carolina. Suzanne enjoys needlework and sewing crafts, and draws inspiration from her three young children.

**Jan Turner**
(pages 60, 61, 62, 63, 64-top, and 67-top) owns and operates Honeysuckle Hollow, a specialty gift shop, with her husband in Hendersonville, North Carolina.

Barbara McIntosh (page 106), Gladys Murray (page 100-center), Louise Riddle (page 51), Paul Rifkin (page 114), Dot Rosenstengel (pages 34-bottom, 35-bottom, and 107-left), Doris Neisler (pages 34-bottom and 35-top and bottom), Linda Seward (pages 100 and 101), Sally Smith (page 76-center top), Elaine Thompson (64-bottom), Nancy Tucker (pages 40-bottom, 41-bottom, 42-left, and 129), Dick Weaver (page 77-right), Tommy Wolff (32-bottom, 40, 41, and 97), and Terry Winfield's home room class at Lucy S. Herring School in Asheville, North Carolina (pages 124 and 125).

# INTRODUCTION

No holiday is as visually and ornately celebrated as Christmas, and the joyous manner in which we decorate our homes seems to become more elaborate every year. Christmas is an important religious and social event for a large portion of the world, a holiday of saints as well as a season of anticipation for children young and old. Christmas draws family, friends, and the world closer together in shared warmth, creating an appreciation of harmony and peace, and a joyous hope for all our futures.

For most of us, decorating our homes marks the opening of the holiday season, yet putting up the tree is often the last step involved in designing a special Christmas look. Good design is the basis for successful holiday decor, for creating a room that is every bit as nice as the Christmas rooms showcased in your favorite magazines. All holiday decorating, no matter how simple, should begin with a design, whether you formally commit it to paper or do your planning in your mind. Following is a discussion of six basic elements used by professional designers. Try not to be intimidated as you read through them: they may seem overwhelming on paper but when you look around your home with a pencil, a pad, and these ideas in mind, they

will suddenly make sense and become your creative tools.

Value is the light or darkness of a specific color. Applying value in practical, simplified terms means considering questions like: What areas of this room need brightening up? Where would a white or light-colored wreath be wasted on a light background? Where would a dark-valued swag most effectively provide rich interest without shouting at viewers? You may have to study the room a while and then balance your value choices along with your color choices.

The room on page 10 presented a complicated problem in selecting a position on the value scale. At first glance, it looks like the room would benefit from light ornamentation such as white or brightly colored flowers and wreaths. The room's lighter values are almost overwhelmed by the dark rock walls and wood work. For everyday colors, the home's owner uses red, bright gold, and cream to brighten and warm the room, so we worked with these established values and added metallic accents in red, gold, and silver. These accents spark up the room and reflect the existing light into the dark corners and recesses.

The room on page 54 demonstrates the brighter end of the value scale. To create contrast and

make a strong holiday theme statement, we chose dark green as a backdrop for the light colors that are at the same end of the value scale as the rest of the room. Red was added as an accent, and works well in this pastel room because it's in the same position on the value scale as the green. We also added a few pieces that match the room's value scale to add interest without challenging the fireside focal point. Perhaps the most simplistic use of value can be seen on page 102. The strong use of red (a darker value) in a light blue and white room creates an uncomplicated and effective holiday atmosphere that's sure to enchant any child. Make value work for you by creating contrast and harmonizing visual elements.

Color has been a favored element of artists for centuries, and it's still the perfect tool to stimulate creative juices. The vision of a Christmas tree all decorated in brilliant colors like blue, red, and purple or in a softer palette of pink, peach, and teal makes us feel good. We fall in love with colors frequently, and what better time of year to indulge color impulses than the holiday season? After all, if we make a mistake, we don't have to live with it for years, and successes can be expanded on for year 'round enjoyment. Avoid overwhelming your room with color by making careful selections. The color approaches below should help you plan which colors to use and where to use them. Monochromatic color schemes involve the use of one color with changes in its value or intensity. Pink for instance, can be used in its palest, almost white shade all the way to its deepest, dark magenta tones. Blue works the same way, ranging from ice blue to deep, almost black, midnight blue. Monochromatic color decorating is an especially successful choice in rooms that are neutral in color and value. A neutral, all-gray room, for instance, just sparkles when decorated with the full intensity and value scale of a color like magenta.

Analogous color schemes use two or three colors or hues from the same side of the color spectrum to create cool or warm moods. Green and blue are cool colors; yellow and orange are warm colors; red and violet add some warmth but not as much as colors with the more dominant yellow hue in them. Choosing an analogous palette is a safe way to experiment with strong use of color without risk, although an analogous scheme can look a little contrived if used in too large of an area.

Direct complements are what traditional Christmas colors are all about. In the color wheel, red is opposite green, blue is opposite orange, and so on. In developing a room's color scheme, we can never have too much of one color without seeming to need just a little of its complement. The traditional complements of red and green are always a success for the holidays. It's best to let one color or the other dominate, using the second color as an accent. The room on page 96 shows red as the dominant color, while the fireplace on page 82 uses the red as the accent. Don't rule out the use of non-traditional complement combinations for your holiday home. Now's your chance to feed your color cravings with orange accented with pale blue. Other methods of color selection impose triangles and rectangles over the color wheel; if you're interested in color these theories will make fascinating reading.

Shape is another important consideration in forming your decor. Repeating shapes will give unity to your designs, and varying their sizes adds visual interest. The kitchen on page 20 owes much of its shape inspiration to the eyes on an owl teapot. The garlic wreaths enlarge and imitate the round shape, while the herb wreath echoes the shapes in the plate display. The starwand collection's display board on page 118 repeats the shape of the room's Palladian window's arch, and the star as a symbolic shape was used throughout the home to provide unity. When considering your Christmas projects, look around your room for shapes to emphasize and then repeat them in your designs.

Line, though not as obvious as shape, still helps formulate a room's design. Look around your room for architectural detail lines you may wish to enhance. The flow of a stair railing, the arch of a door, or the criss-cross in a fabric pattern can all be inspirations. Lines communicate concepts to the viewer and relay the designer's personal style. Straight lines show strength, while gently curving lines are more relaxed and convey movement. Jagged lines are the most exciting of all. Look at the lines of your furnishings: do they reflect you? Can you repeat them or would you change your approach to line for the holiday season? Try combining lots of curves with straight, contemporary styles for contrast, or just go with the flow and use the jagged lines of a star to accent your Southwest decor.

Texture is a very interesting element. It can be tangible (felt) or implied (perceived only by the eyes). Texture is a strong element in holiday projects. Consider the contrast in traditional satin and velvet fabrics paired with evergreens and cones. On page 83, dried flowers and herbs were used to modify the texture of the Christmas tree, creating the illusion of a tapestry.

Intermixing textures in a monochromatic color scheme adds interest and forms a lushness all its own when coupled with a very limited value scheme. Use texture freely, contrasting rough with fine, smooth with coarse, and tangible with implied. Printed or tapestry ribbon contrasts well with the smooth shine of holly or magnolia leaves. The lushness of a velvet stocking looks wonderful against a rugged stone fireplace.

Proportions can be used to your distinct advantage when establishing a holiday focal point. Proportion can also be the cause of failure. That great wreath you spent days making may look insignificant above the fireplace in proportion to the scale of the room. Careful planning, a few decisions about what will be the center of interest (the focal point), and frequent measuring are certain to help. If measuring and visualizing don't make you feel secure about your size choices, then try making a mock-up from craft paper or newspaper first.

Your imagination is the final important element of good design. The rooms featured in this book were chosen because of their uniqueness, so it's not likely you will find one that exactly matches your home. Feel free to mix and match or borrow and steal projects from room to room. The best advice is to design and decorate your home in a way that pleases you, suits your lifestyle, and involves only the amount of time you have to spare. Decorating for the holidays should be a joyous family pleasure and not another stressful task. So relax, select a project that you like, and enjoy making it. Substitute materials to suit your needs and preferences, and don't lose a moment's sleep worrying that your project doesn't seem to be coming out exactly like the one in the book: most craft projects take on a life of their own and refuse to become a carbon copy of a picture in a book. Be confident that if your materials are beautiful, the finished project will be also. And never, ever give up on a project that's only half-way finished. Even the most beautiful of completed projects is an ugly duckling at the half-way point. Have a wonderful holiday season…it's truly magic.

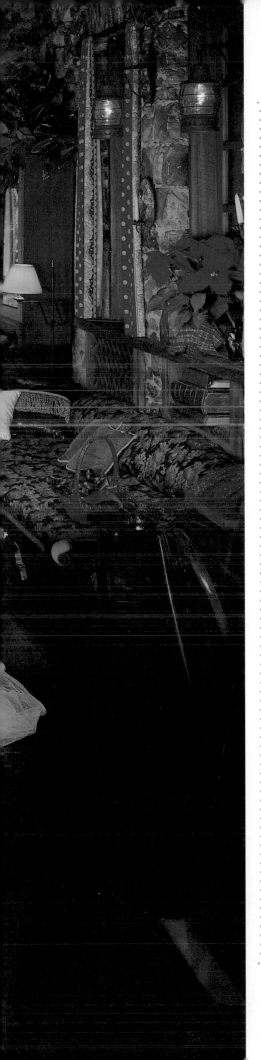

Well known artist Sallie Middleton's home reflects all of the magic and whimsy found in her watercolors, and it's easy to see where she draws her inspiration. The home was built by Sallie's uncle, Douglas Ellenton, a Paris-educated architect who came to the Blue Ridge mountains during a building boom in the 1920s. Constructed with materials such as tile, marble, chestnut, and stone from his municipal building projects, the house was designed around a log cabin that had been on the property since the mid-1800s. The result is an interesting variety of styles, textures, and materials, and a home with all the enchanting allure of an Old World castle.

As her children grew up, Sallie began a tradition of decorating with the fresh materials she gathered in the woods around her home. Holly, hemlock, sprigs of yew, and red berries were arranged into displays throughout the house. In keeping with this tradition, we chose similar forest colors and materials for many of the crafts.

A straightforward design approach seemed the best of many options. The craft projects were designed to highlight the magical elements already in the home. A collection of small gnomes that had been playfully tucked into the stonework of the fireplace wall, for example, became the backdrop for glittering papier-mâché ornaments that bobbed over the gnomes' hiding places. Symbolic motifs such as the sun, moon, and stars were repeated on several of the crafts, and the rich glitter of gold was added whenever possible to emphasize the room's strong sense of history and fantasy.

## Fireplace Screen

The picturesque scene on this tin-punch fireplace screen glistens with lights and intrigue when displayed in front of a fire or in a window. Part of the allure of the screen is its antique finish, which can be achieved with a series of simple techniques.

### Materials

Piece of aluminum flashing measuring 1 x 7-1/2 feet (.3 x 2.3 m.), can of flat black aerosol metal primer, red spray paint, enamel paint in green, brown, white, yellow, and red, wood stain, sand, corrugated cardboard, wood, screws, brads, and nails as indicated in the pattern diagram on pages 140 and 141.

### Tools

Awl, glue gun, saw, hammer, vise, lint-free rag, 1-inch (2.5 cm.) brush

### Instructions

Cut the aluminum into three sections. Enlarge and trace the line drawing for each section onto a piece of tissue paper. Posi-

tion the tissue on top of the aluminum with a piece of corrugated cardboard on the bottom. Use the awl to pierce the aluminum along the drawing lines with about 1/4 of an inch (2/3 cm.) between each punch.

Complete all three sections and then cut the arch at the top of the tin with a pair of scissors. Trim off the excess on the side sections as indicated on the pattern. Build a wood backing for the screen, following the specs on the diagram. Paint the base and the half rounds, referring to the photograph for colors. Allow to dry thoroughly.

Working on one small area at a time, brush on a coat of wood stain and wipe it off with a lint-free rag. Spray the aluminum panels with a layer of matte black paint, working outdoors on a day without wind.

Paint the designs with enamel paint following the colors indicated in the photo and allow to dry completely.

Sprinkle a layer of coarse sand over the enamel-painted areas, leaving some very small places exposed, and sprinkle a light layer over the background areas. Spray the entire screen with red paint. When the paint is almost dry, shake off the sand, rubbing off any remaining sand with your finger tips.

When the red paint has dried completely, mist all the panels with a very light coat of the flat black paint to achieve an antique effect, moving the can back and forth with a constant motion and using short bursts of paint from the can. Do not overdo. Allow to dry completely before moving.

Attach the tin panels to the frame. Tack one half round over the top of the tins and into the frame using the brads, holding in position with a small amount of hot glue. Touch up the brads with paint. Last, hot-glue the wood discs into position and then glue the arches onto the front and back of the tins at the top.

## Papier-Mâché Ornaments

These magical ornaments spin and sparkle in the firelight, and can also be used to brighten the Christmas tree, gift packages, or to fill a crystal bowl.

### Materials

Foam balls in desired size, glue gun, metallic thread or string, package of instant papier-mâché, tubes of acrylic paint in colors of your choice, freezer weight plastic bags, plastic wrap, tube of gold fabric paint, small bells

### Instructions

Hot-glue a loop of thread or string to the top of the foam ball to form a hanger. Mix several batches of papier-mâché in plastic freezer bags as directed on the package and add enough acrylic paint to each bag to achieve the desired colors.

Squeeze out a small amount of the papier-mâché mixture onto a piece of plastic wrap and work it into a triangle, rectangle, or a square that's 1/8 of an inch (1/3 cm.) thick. Fold the plastic up and over the papier-mâché shape and mold the edges until they're straight.

Place the shape against the top of the ball and continue making new shapes and adding them to the ball until the top of the ball is completely covered. Allow to dry completely and then repeat on the other side of the ball. Decorate the areas where the shapes touch with metallic fabric paint as shown in the photo to create a crazy quilt look.

Form small crescent moons, suns, stars, and planets from the papier-mâché mixture and glue them to a length of metallic thread. Glaze the shapes with paint and then glue the thread to the bottom of the ornament as shown in the photo.

## Magic Sleigh

All aboard for a magical ride over snow-filled banks and up into a star-filled sky. A red velvet pillow, gold tassels, and craft jewels add sparkle, and the sleigh is just waiting for someone with enough imagination to go for a ride.

### Materials

Screws and wood as indicated on the pattern diagram on pages 142 and 143, green and red paint, fine sandpaper, gold paint pen, concentrated Liquigems green artist color, walnut wood stain, metallic pipe cleaners, old brass drawer pulls, costume jewelry, gold braid, tassels, plastic gems, red pillow

### Instructions

Cut and assemble the sleigh as shown in the diagram. Fill and sand holes. Paint the sleigh green and then trim the edges in red. To give the sleigh an antique look, sand the painted surface lightly when it's completely dry; then brush the stain onto one board at a time and wipe gently with a rag. When the paint has dried, decorate the sleigh with jewels, tassels, rope braid, and a red velvet pillow.

## Evergreen Spray

Sprays are a lovely alternative to traditional door wreaths and often are less time-consuming to make. The materials in this spray were chosen for their woodland look.

### Materials

Block of floral foam, floral pins, Spanish moss, floral picks, glue gun, paper bow, dried eucalyptus, canella berries, wheat, and preserved cedar

### Instructions

Prepare the base by cutting the block of floral foam into a 5- x 12-inch (12- x 30-cm.) rect-angle. Cover the front and sides of the base with Spanish moss using floral pins. Position the wheat in place and secure with floral pins and a few dabs of hot glue.

Next, hot-glue the bow in place at the same angle as the wheat. Attach the stems of cedar and eucalyptus to floral picks and insert into the foam until you're satisfied with the fullness. Last, hot-glue short stems of canella berries into the spray.

### Materials

Wooden form in ball or egg shape*, wooden candle holder*, water-color pencils (1 each in red, white, blue, grey, pink, flesh, light brown, black), gold glitter paint in squeeze bottle, black colored pencil in non-water soluble for-mula, gold metallic cord, tiny bells, wooden napkin rings* or wooden wheels*, old cane, glue gun, #4 pointed water-color brush, aerosol high gloss acrylic sealer, tracing/ carbon paper, #2 pencil, tape

*Available in a craft store.

## Santa Canes

Antique canes have be-come highly collectible and thus difficult to find, but you can make your own antique replicas with less expense and lots of fun. The finish on these Santa canes gives them an aged appearance, and the canes look great hanging on the wall or stacked upright.

## Instructions

Choose a Santa illustration and enlarge it to fit your wooden cane top. Trace the pattern onto tissue with a #2 pencil. Ease the tissue around the top, clipping the edges of the tissue as needed to make it fit.

Trace over the lines so that the pencil marks transfer to the ball. (Or, slide a small piece of carbon paper under the tissue and trace.) Reverse the tissue on the ball, penciled side down, and tape in place. Remove the tissue and retrace over the lines on the ball with the black colored pencil.

Color the face by rouging the cheeks, placing white highlights on the nose and lips, and then shading the sides of the face and nose. Work with the lightest colors first and progress through the darker ones. When the face is completed, blend the colors with the tip of a slightly damp brush, working with one area at a time and cleaning the

brush between areas.

When dry, re-apply colored pencil in places where the wood shows through and blend again with a damp brush. (If a two-sided cane top is desired, repeat the procedure on the back.) Allow to dry completely and decorate with gold glitter glasses and other details if desired.

Allow the cane top to dry completely and fix with several coats of high gloss acrylic sealer. Drill a tap hole in the ball and cane. Screw one end of a double-ended screw into the cane (holding with pliers), and then turn on the cane top. Position a wooden napkin ring or wheel (painted if desired) to serve as a spacer between the top and the cane.

## Tips

Expensive brushes are worth the extra money in the frustration they'll save you.

Discarded antique chair legs make ideal cane legs.

15

large areas and details around the eye. Create full-size templates with a sizing copy machine, increasing the percentage of reproduction until it's the desired size.

## Santa Rug

Deceptively simple to make, this showstopper rug requires little or no painting skills and takes just a few hours to make. The rug is a perfect way to add Christmas colors and warmth to hardwood floors or to protect your carpeting from those inevitable food spills during holiday parties.

### Materials

Prepared cotton duck, acrylic artist paint (1 tube each of titanium white, brilliant orange, cadmium red medium, ultramarine blue, permanent green deep, mars black), 1/4-inch (.65-cm.) grid tracing paper, glue gun, brushes (round and flat heads), black paint pen, pencil, yard stick, scissors, aerosol acrylic spray

### Instructions

Using the photo of the rug as a reference, copy the pattern onto grid tracing paper, outlining the

Begin painting, saving the eyes, lips, and stars for last. The hat ball and fur are white; the beard and hair are white with a tiny touch of orange;

are white with extra red; and the stars are undercoated with white over the blue sky.

After all the paint has dried, use a black paint pen to sharpen the outline of the nose and eye. Next, add highlights to the tree with green, white, and a touch of orange. Leave overnight to dry, and then cut the canvas in a circle, leaving at least 2 inches (5 cm.) for the hem. To hem, cut canvas as shown in top right photo, fold back, and hot-glue along pencil circle outline.

**Tips**

Spraying the entire canvas with a coat of clear acrylic spray makes clean-up as simple as a quick wipe with a damp sponge. After the holidays, simply roll the canvas up and store in a gift wrap paper tube until next year.

the skin tone is white with tiny touches of red and orange; the rouge color in the cheek is white with a touch of red; the end of the nose is white with red; the lips

## Candle Shelf Wreaths

Using two smaller wreaths instead of a traditional big wreath allows you to create a well-balanced look for a large central focal point. These wreaths were designed with decorated shelves that serve as candle holders.

### Materials

3/4- x 14-inch (2- x 36-cm.) round of plywood, fresh or preserved boxwood, dried pepper berries, red peppers, Billie buttons, German statice, Spanish moss, eucalyptus pods, and poppy seed heads, 60-inch (152-cm.) length of inch-wide (2-1/2-cm.) wired ribbon, glue gun, two 2-inch (5-cm.) wood screws

### Instructions

Following the dimensions and shape indicated in the illustration, cut out the center of the plywood. The large circle will serve as the wreath's base, and the smaller, remaining circle will be the wreath's shelf. Secure the shelf by attaching the smaller circle to the flat area of the wreath base with screws at a 90 degree angle. Cover the wreath base and shelf with Spanish moss using hot glue, leaving a small bare spot on top of the shelf for the candle holder to rest on. Decorate the wreath base by hot-gluing the boxwood and other dried materials into the moss.

### Tips

Decorating the shelf front with the most colorful materials will help draw attention to it.

When hanging your wreath, be sure to leave enough clearance so the candle flame won't burn the wall or ceiling and never leave the flame burning unattended.

5 inches (12 cm)

The lush, simple arrangement on top of the china cabinet, pictured at lower left, works particularly well in rooms with high ceilings. The arrangement was created by overlapping stems of magnolia leaves from the left and right sides and tucking in the remaining natural materials — yarrow, hydrangea, and eucalyptus — instead of using a formal container.

## Materials

Oval-shaped basket or bowl, small block of floral foam, adhesive floral tape, Spanish moss, floral pins, floral picks, dried wheat, roses, yarrow, caspia, lilies, and wild mushrooms

## Instructions

Prepare the basket or bowl by cutting a block of floral foam with a serrated knife to fit inside the bowl. Position the wheat on top of the foam and hold in place with several floral pins. Then secure the foam base and wheat in place by wrapping several times with adhesive floral tape. (See page 157 for instructions on preparing an arrangement's base.) Attach floral picks to all of the dried materials except the yarrow. Cut the yarrow stems at a sharp angle for easier insertion into the foam. Begin arranging by picking a background of caspia into the foam. Follow with the roses, lilies, and mushrooms.

## Forest Centerpiece

The natural allure of fresh mushrooms and the exotic form of dried lilies provided the inspiration for this table arrangement. The red roses, golden yarrow, and rich-toned sage and eucalyptus provide color while reinforcing the room's woodland theme.

## Tips

Although dried mushrooms can be found in some larger craft stores, you can always experiment with drying the mushrooms you find on nature walks or even in your backyard. Just insert the pointed end of a floral pick into the underside of the mushroom and place in an upright position to dry.

The primitive, Old World quality of this kitchen provides a welcome setting for a collection of custom twig birdhouses, and the intimate cooking area begs to help create culinary craft gifts like homemade herbal vinegars, butters, jellies, cookies, and fresh breads.

The unique patterned brick walls, antique tavern table, and massive wood doors create a sophisticated contrast to the delicate collection of antique china. The simplicity of the projects such as the garlic and pepper wreaths and matching garland were chosen to reinforce this simple elegance.

Even if you have a formal dining room, the intimacy and warmth of a kitchen is ideal for small Christmas gatherings. Dim the lights, decorate with lots of candles and homemade crafts, and look forward to an evening of friendship and laughter in somewhat unconventional surroundings.

## Tips

Farmers markets and food wholesalers often have much better prices than grocery stores on garlic and peppers.

## Garlic Wreaths

A natural combination, garlic and peppers work just as well together in wreaths as they do in a garland. The wreaths can remain hanging after the holidays or be packed away for next year's decorations.

### Materials

16-inch (41-cm.) foam wreath base, 3-inch (7-cm.) wooden floral picks, garlic bulbs, red peppers, Spanish moss, glue gun

### Instructions

Arrange the garlic bulbs around the wreath base and secure in place by inserting a floral pick through each bulb and down into the base. Reinforce each bulb with a dab of hot glue.

## Garlic Garland

Garlic, wild mushrooms, and red peppers add lovely culinary accents to a base of woodland materials. A winter walk in the woods can provide you with inspiration and materials.

### Materials

Preserved cedar, dried eucalyptus, fern, mushrooms, and canella berries, garlic bulbs, spool wire, thin-gauge wire, glue gun

### Instructions

Measure the area where you plan to hang the garland and cut a length of spool wire to fit. Then trim the stems of cedar, eucalyptus, and fern to approximately 8 inches (20 cm.) and arrange them in small bouquets of six stems each.

Hold a single bouquet against the base wire and secure by wrapping several times with thin-gauge wire. Position the next bouquet so it overlaps the stems of the previous bouquet and wire in place. Continue wiring bouquets until the entire length of the base is covered. Last, use a glue gun to add the accent materials — garlic bulbs, stems of canella berries, and dried mushrooms — into the garland.

After the surface area of the wreath base has been covered, fill in the spaces between the garlic bulbs with Spanish moss. Finish decorating by hot-gluing red peppers around the wreath.

## Gift Basket

What better way to surprise friends and family during the holiday season than a

custom-decorated gift basket filled with homemade vinegars, jellies, and herb butters? The woodland and culinary theme makes the basket a pretty kitchen decoration until it's given.

### Materials

Basket, glue gun, raffia, preserved cedar, reindeer moss, wild mushrooms, eucalyptus, canella berries, red peppers

### Instructions

Trim the cedar to 4-inch (10-cm.) lengths and hot-glue around the rim of the basket. Hot-glue the remaining materials into the cedar, saving the berries and peppers for last.

Cut five lengths of raffia to 12 inches (30 cm.) and hot-glue to the top of the basket's handle. Hot-glue berries, peppers, and small chunks of moss on top of the raffia and the handle. Finish decorating by hot-gluing small stems of eucalyptus, mushrooms, moss, and berries along the handle.

## Mr. & Mrs. Claus's Boot Rack

Finally! Here's a fun place to hang those messy winter boots. The rack is simple to construct and can be custom designed to fit your family's needs.

### Materials

One piece of pine 1x10x23 inches (2.5x25x57 cm.), 1 piece of pine 1x6x23 inches (2.5x15x57 cm.), 3 2-inch (5-cm.) "L" brackets, 12 half-inch (1-1/4 cm.) wood screws, 7 1-1/2-inch (4-cm.) wood screws, water base craft paint (1 container each in white, red, green, and gold), paint pens (1 pen each in red, green, gold, black, and blue), tracing

paper, carbon paper, wood stain, fine sandpaper, white wood glue

### Tools

Scissors, saber saw, electric drill, screwdriver, paint brushes, rag

### Instructions

Using the boots you plan to hang as a pattern, trace their outline onto a piece of cardboard around the heel of the boot to the ball of the foot section. Draw a line 1-inch (2.5 cm.) inside the tracing on the boots' sides and erase the original line. Cut out the cardboard and use it as a pattern to trace onto the 1x10. Turn the cardboard over and trace again for the opposite foot's shape. Space the cutouts evenly as shown in the photo. Cut 1/2 inch (1 1/4 cm.) radius corners at the tops ends of the 1x6 and the

1x10 as shown in the photo and sand to round the edges. Paint all the wood white and allow to dry completely. Trace the patterns shown on the bottom of page 23 onto sheets of tissue paper.

Position the tracing onto the wood as shown in the photo of the rack above. Slide a sheet of carbon paper under the tissue, tape the tissue in place, and trace over the pattern to transfer the design onto the wood.

When all of the designs have been transferred into the correct position, outline them with paint pens and fill in with craft paint. Add the berry dots last. (Note: The snowflake is made by just connecting straight lines.)

When you've finished painting, sand over the painting lightly to create an antique appearance, creating wear marks where they would logically occur. Brush on a layer of wood stain and wipe lightly with a rag to complete the antique look.

Working along an imaginary line 3/8 of an inch (1 cm.) in from the back of the board, drill tap holes through the bottom and into the top 1 inch from the left edge and every 3-1/2 inches (8

cm.) thereafter to make seven holes in all. Screw the two sections together using white glue in the joints. Reinforce by adding "L" brackets between boots and boot pairs. Hang by screwing through the back into a door or plaster wall.

## Christmas Moon Rug

This festive kitchen rug catches drips and spills from holiday baking yet easily wipes clean because it's been sprayed with several coats of acrylic spray. The design was created with stencils purchased in a craft store and the moon pattern from the drawing on page 29.

**Materials**
Prepared cotton duck canvas cut to desired size with a 2-inch (5-cm.) hem allowance on all sides, purchased Christmas stencil of your choice, paint brushes (one stencil brush and three flat-headed brushes in sizes 1/4 inch, 1 inch, and 3 inch, (.65 cm., 2.5 cm., 7 cm.), black paint pen, carbon paper, hot glue, pencil, acrylic paints (1 tube each of titanium white, brilliant orange, blue, red, permanent green deep, mars black, and yellow)

**Instructions**
Beginning at the top of the canvas, brush on a layer of water-thinned paint. Brush with parallel, horizontal strokes to give the background color a graduated look. Don't be concerned about streaking; it will only enhance the rug's character.

24

When the background color is completely dry, arrange the stencils at the base of the rug as shown in the photo. It's probably best to trace them lightly in pencil first to make sure you like their placement.

Using a stencil brush and green or red acrylic paint, begin dabbing in the paint. Use a small brush in small areas and a larger brush in larger areas. Find the crescent moon drawing on page 29 and enlarge it to fit your design size. Tape the enlargement onto the pre-painted background. Slide carbon paper underneath and trace over

the outside outline with a pencil. Fold back the carbon paper and enlargement but do not remove.

Paint in the traced moon area with white paint. Draw random stars in the sky and paint them in with white paint. When dry, return the tracing to its original position and finish tracing the details inside the moon. Remove the tape and carbon paper carefully to prevent damage to the painting.

14-inches (10 cm.)

←— 6 inches (15 cm.) —→

Paint the stars with yellow paint using a small flat-headed brush. Paint inside the moon with a larger brush, following the colors shown in the photo and shading as you would if you were applying make-up. A black paint pen can help you master the detail work. When the canvas is completely dry, turn under a 2-inch hem, mitering all corners to fit and securing with hot glue. Seal with several coats of acrylic spray.

### Tips
Flip and flop the stencils around the rug to add symmetry and interest to your design. Use the same stencil to make matching place mats.

## Herb Wreath
This kitchen wreath makes a clever way to store your summer harvest of culinary herbs. The fabric pounces are held to the base with elastic cords so they can be removed quickly for additions to your favorite meals, and the pouches are lined with plastic bags to keep the herbs fresh.

### Materials
Oval grapevine wreath base, preserved magnolia leaves, dried eucalyptus, unbleached muslin, cardboard, several colors of puff paint, small plastic bags, elastic cording in red, green, and gold, glue gun, paper ribbon, plastic wire beads

### Instructions
Cut out the sachet bags by following the pattern at the bottom of the page. Sew the sides and bottom shut with a 1/2-inch (1-1/4-cm.) seam allowance and fray the top edge if desired. Slide a piece of cardboard inside the bags and decorate the front of each bag with puff paint.

Fill each plastic bag with a different dried herb. The herbs can be purchased in bulk from health food stores or picked fresh from a summer garden, washed, and spread on a paper towel to dry. Tie the bags shut with red or green elastic cord and then tie them to the wreath base with the gold cord.

Fill in the remaining space on the wreath by hot-gluing in magnolia leaves and dried eucalyptus. Meander a length of paper ribbon and plastic wire beads around the wreath, securing with hot-glue as needed. Tie the ribbon into a bow at the top.

## Peanut Bird Tree

This magical tree houses an enchanting collection of peanut birds. Each bird is truly an individual, with a look and personality all its own. This project is an ideal way to spend a cold winter night in front of the television.

### Materials

Large bag of unroasted peanuts, gold aerosol paint, several colors of puff fabric paint, small tree (artificial or fresh), straight sewing pins, cardboard, small plastic or glass beads

### Instructions

Working outdoors, arrange a flat layer of peanuts in a cardboard box and spray with gold paint. Allow to dry. Turn each peanut over and spray again.

Prepare the peanuts for decorating by placing each one in an upright position on a sheet of cardboard with the small end facing up. Secure the peanuts in place by inserting a sewing pin up through the bottom of the cardboard and into the shell.

Decorate the peanuts by squeezing a small amount of paint at the small end of each peanut and pulling away to form the beak. After the beak dries, squeeze a dot on each side to form the eyes and press a small bead into the paint while it's still wet. Finish decorating by adding wings, scarfs, hats, or anything else you like.

### Tips

Don't try to decorate each peanut in exactly the same colors and shapes or to predetermine what it will look like; just squeeze the paint and let it create the characters for you.

Be sure to warn children (and adults!) not to eat the peanuts after they've been decorated.

## Star Candles

Light up your holidays with these star candles shaped with metal cookie cutters. A coordinated table centerpiece can be made by arranging some greenery around a plate of decorated matching star cookies.

### Materials

Metal star-shaped cookie cutters, candle wick, candle wax, aerosol gold glitter paint, non-stick cooking spray

### Instructions

Line a cookie pan with a protective layer of aluminum foil. Arrange the cookie cutters flat on the pan and spray with a protective layer of cooking spray.

Pour melted candle wax into each cookie cutter until about half full. Add the wax slowly to help seal the bottom edge where the cutter and pan meet. Allow the wax to set until slightly firm; then position the wick on top of the wax and fill the remaining space with melted wax. When the candles are completely hardened, remove them from the cookie cutters and spray with a layer of gold glitter paint.

## Folk Art Birdhouse Fantasies

Ordinary birdhouses make perfect homes for your peanut birds when they've been decorated with some greenery, fabric paint, and a whimsical imagination. The houses make unusual table centerpieces, add cheer to small corner tables, and look nice under the Christmas tree.

### Materials

Basic plywood birdhouse, sheet moss, glue gun, twigs, 1-inch (2-1/2 - cm.) nails, small piece of vine, tube of opalescent white acrylic paint, one decorated peanut bird, sewing pins, small plastic bells, and snowflakes from a craft store

### Instructions

Beginning with the roof, cover the outer surface area of the birdhouse with moss using hot glue. (The moss can be attached in pieces if necessary.) Cut the twigs and tack in position, starting with the top as shown in the photo on page 28. Create a perch with thin vine and tack or glue in place.

Spread a protective layer of newspaper under the birdhouse. Create the illusion of snow by squeezing the tube paint over the twigs. (Be generous with the paint because it will shrink as it dries.)

Use sewing pins to attach the gold bells, and hot-glue the snowflakes and peanut bird to the front of the house.

# Folk Art Birdhouse Church

## Materials

Plywood base approximately 4 x 12 inches (10 x 30 cm.), twigs, papier-mâché, small nails, sheet moss, very small amount of water-based black paint, small pieces of fern or greenery, glue gun, red glass beads, narrow red ribbon, small pinecone craft novelty, tube of red fabric paint, red pipe cleaner

beads into the greenery. Create a doorway with small twigs and nail in place. Then decorate the door by gluing greenery and red ribbon in place, finishing with a miniature pinecone spray at the top. Paint any nail heads that show with red fabric paint.

## Instructions

Cut the twigs into 2-inch (5-cm.), 4-inch, 10-inch (25-cm.), and 12-inch segments. Arrange the twigs on the bottom of the base and nail in place. Build the walls of the house up like a log cabin. When you reach the roof, cut twigs to fit under the eaves and nail in at an angle. Arrange the roof logs and nail in place.

Tuck pieces of sheet moss between the roof logs.

Prepare a papier-mâché mixture in a plastic bag with warm water and enough black paint to color shown in the photo. Squeeze the mixture together until it becomes the right consistency, and then use it to fill in the spaces between the logs. Wipe off any excess with a damp sponge.

Decorate the house with a garland made from small pieces of greenery and glue the glass

Create a miniature wreath with small pieces of greenery and glue in place. Then create the illusion of berries by dabbing small amounts of red fabric paint in the greenery. Last, form a cross with a pipe cleaner and hot-glue it to the top of the house.

## Moss Covered Birdhouse

### Materials
Basic plywood birdhouse, sheet moss, glue gun, twigs, small nails, 1 tube each of yellow and red fabric paint, plastic white beads, white thread, miniature decorated wreath from a craft store, glitter pipe cleaners

### Instructions
Beginning with the roof, cover the outer surface area of the birdhouse with moss using hot glue. (The moss can be attached in pieces if necessary.) Cut the twigs and tack in position, starting with the top as shown in the photo on page 28. Create a perch with thin vine and tack or glue in place.

Decorate the roofline by making loops in the pipe cleaner and hot-gluing in place. String the beads on a piece of thick thread and hot-glue in place to look like a strand of lights. Position the wreath on the front of the house and hot-glue in place. Last, add festive color to the house with dots of red and yellow fabric paint.

### Tip
Your favorite arrangement of collectibles becomes a festive part of the room when decorated with a few sprigs of greenery. Cinnamon sticks, berries, and small tree ornaments can be added for a more elaborate arrangement.

For many years, artists Jo Lydia and Ian Craven lived on the Costa del Sol in Southern Spain and later in France's Loire Valley. The impact of these picturesque locations on their work, their lifestyle, and the interior design of their home is very apparent.

We've chosen to echo this colorful style in the holiday projects designed for this room. Drawing from the Cravens' patterns and palette, we used brightly-colored tassels, braids, and fabrics. We've even printed kilim-style place mats in holiday colors to match the marvelous antique rugs.

The porcelain ornaments, vases, plates, and other pieces of pottery created by Jo Lydia and Ian are often embellished with the intricacies of antique lace imprints before they're glazed to a shiny opalescent finish.

The ornaments on page 45 are an imitation of Jo Lydia's design, but are made from an inexpensive and easy-to-work-with modeling compound that is imprinted with patterns from cloth or paper doilies. The influence of their porcelain textures can also be seen in the pinecone lamp and Santa frame in this chapter and the pinecone candle holders in the following chapter.

## Victorian Santa Frame and Swag

This elaborate Victorian approach to framing makes a perfect fireplace swag to decorate your mantel or to hang above a door as a focal point if you have high ceilings.

### Materials

14-inch (36-cm.) foam wreath base, 2- x 12- x 8-inch (5- x 27- x 20-cm.) foam oval (see pattern on page 147), 2 dowels 1/4-inch (2/3 cm.) wide and 3 inches (7 cm.) long, a Santa portrait 5 inches (12 cm.) in diameter, clear acetate, assortment of seed pods, heads, and cones (about half a grocery bag full), 2 dried pomegranates, heavy-gauge wire, uncorrugated scrap cardboard, gold gild paint, paint brush, glue gun

### Instructions

Use a serrated knife to cut the foam wreath base in half. Trim the ends on a diagonal so they fit firmly against the oval center base. Cut a piece of cardboard to reinforce the joint between the foam arches (wreath) and the oval foam base.

Insert the wood dowels through the wreath arches and the oval foam at the connecting point. Remove the dowels, apply glue to their tips, and reinsert. Add a little hot glue as you're pushing the foam pieces together and allow to dry. Turn the foam pieces over and hot-glue scraps of cardboard to cover the joint. Shave the foam ends down to a flat point with a serrated knife.

Working from both ends of the arches, position the cones, pods, and seed heads to form a balanced design on both ends of the swag. Begin gluing, remembering to work alternately on both ends to ensure uniformity. (Note: You may need to wire the heavier cones or pods into position first and then reinforce with hot glue.)

Begin working on the oval centerpiece by outlining a 5-inch circle where Santa's portrait will be located with a pencil. Arrange the center top and bottom design but don't glue yet.

Cut the points off the cones you plan to use on the sides. Hot-glue the outer edges of cones, working inward and varying the cones' heights so they fit snugly on top of each other. Stop gluing before you get close to the portrait's outline.

Position and glue Santa's portrait. Place the acetate on top of the photo and protect the acetate with a piece of tissue paper. Continue gluing the remaining materials, taking care not to glue down the tissue. Gild the cones, pods, pomegranates, and seed heads with a dry brush. Attach a heavy-gauge wire hanger to the center of the oval.

## Tip
If you can't find a portrait of Santa that's just the right size, use a color photocopying service to enlarge a photo from a magazine or greeting card.

## Pine Needle Frame
Easy to construct, this pine needle frame makes a perfect frame for Santa. Since we didn't have a large photo of Santa, we enlarged a color Santa sticker to fit the frame.

### Materials
1/2-inch (1-1/4-cm.) plywood cut in a large oval shape, pine needles, raffia, tapestry needle, craft glue, glue gun, aerosol shellac, easel backing

### Instructions
Place 2 clumps of pine needles against the outer edge of the plywood oval so that about half of the needles overlap. Thread the tapestry needle with a length of raffia and begin stitching the 2 rows of needles together with a chain stitch. (See illustration on page 143.) Follow the curves of the oval and add new clumps of pine needles as needed.

Trim the Santa photo to fit the oval and glue it in place against the wood. Spray the pine needles with shellac and allow to dry completely. Hot-glue the pine needle oval on top of Santa's photo and then hot-glue the easel to the back of the frame.

## Pinecone Lamp Base

Sharing many of the same materials, textures, and painting techniques enables this contemporary lamp base to blend well with the Victorian mantel swag on preceding page.

### Materials

4-inch (10-cm.) wide heavyweight mailing tube cut to 16 inches (41 cm.) in height, grocery bag full of small pinecones, glue gun, hemlock cones, flat black spray paint, turquoise acrylic paint, gold metallic craft paint, old lamp parts or kit, lamp shade

### Instructions

Cut the pointed ends off the pinecones with wire snippers, leaving the bases of the cones in various thicknesses. Starting at the bottom of the tube, begin hot-gluing pinecones all around the base, trimming one side of the cone flush to fit the edge of the tube. Continue gluing cones tightly together until the entire tube is covered. Trim the cones flush with the top edge and fill any blank spaces with miniature hemlock cones.

Spray the entire cylinder with flat black paint. When the paint is thoroughly dry, brush on a coat of turquoise paint, allowing some of the black paint to show through in the deeper crevices. After the paint has dried, create highlights by brushing gold craft paint on the tops of the cones. Assemble the lamp after all paint is thoroughly dry using a kit or parts from an old lamp.

## Fabric Picture Frames

These picture frames are an inexpensive alternative to the customized creations of interior designers. Choose fabrics that blend or match the patterns and colors in your room or opt for fabrics with holiday motifs.

### Materials

Double picture mat set, picture backing easel, sheet of acetate large enough to fit the opening of the mat set, fabric large enough to cover the mat set with a 5/8-inch (1-2/3 cm.) allowance on all sides, double layer of quilt batting, fabric glue

### Instructions

Place the bottom mat from the set face down on the wrong side of your fabric, making sure that any patterns on the fabric are square with the mat. Trace the shape of the mat with a felt tip pen, adding a 5/8-inch wrap allowance on all sides. Use a straight edge to draw a diagonal line through the opening in the mat from each top corner to each bottom corner to form an X.

Remove the mat and cut out the fabric, making sure not to cut too deeply into the diagonal X lines. Replace the mat over the fabric and draw a second line 5/8 of an inch in from the inside edge of the mat all the way around. Cut off the excess fabric along these lines.

Trace the inner and outer edges of the bottom mat onto a double thickness of batting and cut it out. Glue the batting to the front of this mat. Place the fabric right side down and place the batting-covered mat squarely on top of it. Fold over the fabric edges and glue them to the back of the mat.

Using the top mat from the set, cut the top border of the mat to form a U shape. Glue this piece to the back of the fabric-covered mat so that the opened end of the U is to the top or one side. Glue the picture easel to the back of the mat, and slide the photo and acetate through the top of the U.

## Gilded Basket Tray

A golden frosted basket is the perfect place to display fragrant orange pomanders or a bowl of evergreen potpourri. When you're expecting holiday company, line the basket with napkins, fill with snacks, and use the basket as a centerpiece.

### Materials

Willow tray, 2 yards (1.8 m.) of wide gold French ribbon, small and medium pinecones, white paint, gold spray paint, spool wire, glue gun

### Instructions

Spray the willow tray gold and allow to dry complete-ly. Form a bow in the middle of the ribbon and wire it through the bow's loop to the tray. Loop the ribbon for a few inches and wire again to the tray. Twist and loop twice more until both ends meet, wiring as needed. Tie the 2 ends in a loose knot,

wire in position, and allow the streamers to hang over the basket's edge. Whitewash the cones with a dry brush. When the paint has dried, wire the cones together and attach them in small bunches to the tray, concealing the wire that's hold-ing the ribbon in position. Reinforce as needed with hot glue.

## Crazy Patchwork Stocking

on page 37

Developed by pioneer-ing Americans to make use of even the small-est pieces of fabric, this style of patch-work is still popular. In the late 1800s, the Victorians made crazy quilts with lav-ish fabrics like velvet and silk instead of used clothing scraps, and their seams were embroidered with silk floss instead of simple yarn.

### Materials

Fabric scraps that are at least 4 inches (10 cm.) square, 5/8 yard (.6 m.) of muslin or broadcloth (does not show in finished pro-ject), 5/8 yard fabric of your choice for back of stocking, 5/8 yard lining fabric, 2 yards (1.8 m.) of piping for the stocking's edge, several colors of embroi-dery floss (narrow lace trim or ribbon can be substituted)

### Instructions

Trace the pattern on page 155 and cut out 1 stocking of muslin, 1 of the back material, and 2 of the lin-ing. Using the muslin stocking as a guide, begin arranging scrap fabric pieces to establish the end design.

Remember that crazy quilt-ing doesn't require a spe-cific rhyme or reason, just place the scraps wherever you like and trim the sides to fit each other. Begin at either the top or foot of the stocking.

If you plan to embroider along the seams, use a 1/4-inch (2/3-cm.) seam allowance to join the pieces together and secure your work to the base by "stitching in the ditch" (in the center of a seam so the stitches disappear). If you plan to use lace or ribbon trim instead of embroidery, you will only need to baste the pieces to the muslin because the trim will cover the seams.

When all of the pieces are in place, baste from the back 1/2 inch from the edge and trim the excess fabric away from the muslin base. Embroider (or machine sew trims in place) along the seam lines with 2 strands of floss using one of the border stitches shown here or one you've invented. When finished, press on the wrong side while gently stretching.

Position the piping along the seam line of the back fabric and baste in place.

Place front and back stocking pieces right sides together, and stitch in 5/8-inch (1-2/3-cm.) seams. Trim seams to 1/4 inch. Stitch the lining pieces together with a 5/8-inch seam and trim to 1/4 inch.

Place the stocking and lining right sides together and stitch, leaving a 3-inch (7-1/2 cm.) opening in the top edge of the back. Turn the right sides out so the lining is inside the patchwork stocking. Hand-stitch the opening closed and press. Tie a loop and a bow in the ribbon and tack them in place at the top corner of the stocking.

## Crazy Quilt Place Mats

These place mats add a subtle richness to any table. If you find yourself tight on time, just make one and use it as a centerpiece.

### Materials

Fabric scraps that are at least 4 inches (10 cm.) square, 5/8 yard (.6 m.) of muslin or broadcloth (does not show in finished project), 5/8 yard fabric of your choice for back of stocking, 2 yards (1.8 m.) of piping for the stocking's edge, several colors of embroidery floss (narrow lace trim or ribbon can be substituted)

### Instructions

Cut out the muslin base and back fabrics from the pattern on page 153. Using the general techniques described in the stocking directions, cover the muslin with crazy patchwork and then finish the seams with embroidery, lace, or ribbon.

Position the front and back pieces right sides together and sew, leaving an opening 3 inches wide on a straight edge for turning. Turn right sides out, press, and hand-stitch the opening closed.

## Velvet Ornaments

These versatile ornaments can be used as tree ornaments or to dress up a centerpiece on your dining room table.

### Materials

3- or 2-1/2-inch (7- or 6-cm.) foam ball, 3 colors of scrap fabric, piping trim, 2 large sequins in star or flower shapes, large ornament hook, craft glue, sharp-edged knife, string

### Instructions

Trace and cut out the reference star pattern and segment pieces that fit your size ball from the patterns on page 153. Tack the star pattern on the ball with a pin. Beginning at the center of the star, wrap the string around the ball in one direction and trace the string line in pencil. Repeat the above step for the other 2 star lines so you have 6 equal sections.

Check for accuracy by measuring along the widest part of the ball and comparing the distance between the lines. Remove the star and make a small pencil hole at the top of the ball where the lines began and at the bottom of the ball where the lines ended. Use the knife to cut along the lines about 1/4-inch (2/3-cm.) deep. Cut out 2 segments from each of the 3 colors for a total of 6 segments. Center a piece of fabric over a sec-

tion and use the knife to press the seam allowances (1/4 inch) on each side into the cuts you made earlier. Repeat until each segment

is covered with fabric. Cut 6 pieces of piping (or other trim such as rickrack or narrow lace) to fit the segments and press them into the seams with the knife. Adjust the trim if necessary so it looks evenly spaced.

Glue a sequin at the top and bottom of the ball. Straighten the loop out of a large ornament hook and push one end of the wire into the top sequin's hole. Allow all glue to dry completely before hanging.

## Reindeer

Purchased from a craft supplier, this grapevine reindeer can be dressed up every year and used indoors or out. We added length to his antlers by weaving twigs into the vine and reinforcing as needed with hot glue. The reindeer's bridle and reins are made from red and gold ribbon and two gold bells, and a crazy quilt place mat makes a perfect blanket for his back.

## Floral Cornhusk Basket Arrangement

This vibrant symmetrical display of dried flowers brings summer color into your holiday home. You can use flowers dried from last year's garden or purchase materials from a craft store.

### Materials

Horse tail grass, canella berries, Mexican sage, billy buttons, red annual statice, red and white and purple globe amaranth, yarrow, red pepper berries, 2 yards (1.8 m.) of red cording, block of foam, floral tape, heavy-gauge floral wire to lengthen short stems, glue gun

### Instructions

Tie the cording in a bow and glue it to the basket. Cut the foam with a serrated knife to fit securely inside the basket 1 inch (2-1/2 cm.) below the rim. Determine the center of the arrangement and score a straight line from the front to the back to divide the foam into 2 equal halves.

Cut the horse tail grass to 13-inch (33-cm.) lengths. Begin the arrangement by inserting a row of horse tail 1 inch into the foam down the center line. Glue individual canella berries to the tops of each length of horse tail. Gather the Mexican sage into groups of 3 stems each and create a 12-inch (30-cm.) stem with floral tape by attaching the stems in each group to wire with floral tape. (See page 156 for general instructions.) Insert the wires an inch into the foam directly in front of the horse tail on both sides.

Use floral tape and wire to lengthen groups of 3 stems of globe amaranth to 10 inches (25 cm.) and insert the stems in front of the Mexican sage an inch into the foam. Cut the billy button stems down to 9-1/2 inches (23 cm.) and insert them an inch into the foam in front of the globe amaranth. Next tape bits of red statice to wire to make 8-inch (20-cm.) stems and insert them an inch deep into the foam in front of the billy buttons.

Trim the yarrow stems to 7 inches (17 cm.) and insert them in front of the statice. Create several additional bunches of Mexican sage with a stem length of 8 inches and insert them in front of yarrow. Assemble the white globe amaranth in groups of 5 or 6 and tape them to wire to form 5-inch stems. Insert these stems snugly in front of the Mexican sage. Finish by filling in the sides of the arrangement

with assorted materials so that no stems show. Position the pepper berries evenly to hang over the edges of the basket and hot-glue in place.

**Tip**
Be sure to finish working on each side of the arrangement with a specific material before going on to a new material.

## Antiqued Country Rooster
Inspired by a country weather vane, this wonderful rooster is adding the final decorating touches to his Christmas tree.

### Materials
Pine board measuring 1 x 10 x 14 inches, (2-1/2 x 25 x 36 cm.), wood base measuring 2 x 3-1/2 x 8 inches (5 x 8 x 20 cm.), piece of pine measuring 1 x 4 x 5 inches (2-1/2 x 10 x 12 cm.), 2 dowels measuring 3/8 x 6 inches (1 x 15 cm.) and 3/8 x 2 inches, 3 inches (7 cm.) of gold cord, 1 small craft star, acrylic paint in red, green, and white, gold paint pen, sandpaper, walnut wood stain

### Instructions
Following the pattern on page 146, trace and cut out the rooster and

Christmas tree. Sand the edges. Paint the rooster and the longest dowel white and allow to dry. Apply a second coat of red paint to the rooster and the dowel and allow to dry.

Paint the Christmas tree, the shortest dowel, and the base green. When the paint has dried, measure off 1-inch squares on the base and paint in a red checkerboard pattern. When the paint has dried, sand some paint off the edges, and wipe on a coat of walnut stain; wait 15 minutes and wipe off the excess stain with a lint-free rag. Repeat the sanding and staining procedure on the Christmas tree, rooster, and dowel. This will give you an antique look.

Draw ornaments on the tree with a gold paint pen. Drill 3/8-inch holes into the base 1-1/2 inches from the edge, centered front to back. Drill corresponding holes in the bottom of the rooster and the tree. Glue the dowels into tree, rooster, and base.

## Braid and Tassel Window Treatment

This project is an easy way to add sparkle to an uncurtained or solid color window treatment for the holidays.

### Materials

Tassels, several yards (2 to 3 m.) of braid, gold metallic pipe cleaners, floral wire, 3-inch (7-1/2-cm.) pleated French gold ribbon,

wooden closet pole rod to fit length of your window, glue gun

### Instructions

Following the diagram on page 148, lay out the braid and cut to fit. Wire and hot-glue the braid ends together and then glue on the tassels. Wrap the pipe cleaners over the tassels to conceal the glue. Attach additional pipe cleaners to loop over the rod and wrap the pipe cleaners over the braid as indicated on pattern.

Begin to wrap your pole from one end to the other, allowing an extra 18 inches (46 cm.) of ribbon overhang on both ends. Glue the ribbon in place and form bows at both ends. Attach the braided tassels to the rod with the pipe cleaners. Finish by laying the rod on top of an existing rod or by putting up wooden brackets for the rod.

## Paper Cutwork Pictures

Made from the ancient German paper cutting craft known as scherenschnitte, these holiday pictures will make great gifts for everyone on your list.

### Materials

Colored stationery or parchment paper, cutting pattern from page 148, tissue and carbon paper, tape, short sharp-pointed scissors or craft knife, glue stick, watercolors or coffee, mat board or frame

### Instructions

Transfer the cutting pattern of your choice onto the paper. If your paper is translucent, you can simply trace it. If the paper is too dark or too thick to trace, you will need to transfer it by first tracing the pattern onto tissue paper. Then place the carbon paper face down on the cutting paper and place the tissue face down on top of the carbon paper. Now outline the pattern showing through the tissue paper with a pencil.

Fold the paper as indicated on the pattern and tape the sides with small pieces of tape to prevent shifting during cutting. Begin cutting at the center of the design with the most detailed part of the design and work outward.

Press the finished paper with a warm iron to remove creases and wrinkles. Create an aged look by sponging on diluted coffee, or paint with watercolors if desired. Finish by gluing the cutout onto a piece of contrasting mat board and then by framing.

## Santa Collections

These fun Santas can be purchased unpainted from your local craft store, and painting them makes a great family tradition. Be sure to have everyone sign and date the Santas every year so you can enjoy watching the progression of skills through the years.

**Materials**
Purchased pre-cast resin Santas, tubes of acrylic paint, pointed brushes in various sizes

**Instructions**
Paint as your imagination and whimsies dictate.

**Tip**
Create an antique look by brushing on a coat of provincial stain and then rubbing off the excess with a dry, lint-free rag.

# Firewood Storage Box

This antiqued wood storage chest makes a wonderful place for storing firewood in the winter and garden tools in the summer. Although the box looks nice on a porch, it has been sized to work as an end table for use next to a sofa if desired.

## Materials

4 lengths of 1- x 12- x 38-inch (2-1/2- x 30- x 96-cm.) wood for the front, bottom, and backboards, 2 lengths of 1- x 12- x 17-inch (2-1/2- x 30- x 43-cm.) wood for sides, 1- x 12- x 37-inch wood for the top, 1- x 1-1/4- x 38-inch wood stripping, number 6 finishing nails or old square-headed nails, purchased ball-shaped wooden legs (optional), country red latex paint, provincial stain, sandpaper

## Tools

Nail set, hammer, saw

## Instructions

Use the patterns on page 144 to cut out the wood. Nail the stripping onto the lid, making sure that the same amount of stripping over- hangs on each side. Nail the front piece to the sides.

Cut out the pattern at the top of the backboards and nail the 2 back- boards to the front and sides. Nail on the bottom. Sand all pieces and make any necessary adjustments to the lid. Set the nails (unless you've used square heads). Fill the nail holes and sand smooth.

Screw purchased wooden balls (or make your own by carving tapered, 2-inch legs from 2 x 4s) into the inside corners. You may opt instead to let the bin sit flat on the floor.

Paint the entire chest country red. Sand the edges to wear away some of the paint. Brush on a coat of provincial stain and wipe off the excess with a dry lint-free rag.

Left to right: Amanda, Susie, Emma Lou, and Maximillian, who traveled with their owners from Spain to America on the Queen Elizabeth II, sit in front of a 17th-century Normandy headboard. The center doors of this unique piece slide open at night to expose a bed, and the pillows and blankets store in the forward bench seat during the day.

## Lace-Embossed Clay Tree Ornaments

These quick and easy ornaments will cover your tree in beautiful lace patterns and can be painted to the color of your choice if desired.

### Materials

Modeling compound clay, luncheon-size plate, masking tape, pieces of old lace or paper doilies, talcum powder, 1- x 8-inch (2-1/2- x 20 cm.) dowel rod, cocktail-size straw, gold or silver thread

### Instructions

Tape the luncheon plate face down onto a protected work surface and lightly dust with talcum powder. Using the dowel rod, roll a 1-inch ball to an even thickness in the center of the plate.

Place the lace over the clay and roll again to emboss the pattern in the clay. Remove the lace and push the cocktail straw into the top of the ornament to form a hanging hole. Bake the clay according to manufacturer's instructions.

Make hangers for the ornaments with the metallic thread.

# Faux Victorian Feather Tree

The elegant, geometric lines of this tree make it the ideal place to display a collection of handmade ornaments. Stems of pampas grass were used instead of the traditional feathers because they make the tree less expensive and easier to construct.

## Materials

1- x 1- x 30-inch (2-1/2- x 2-1/2- x 75-cm.) wood strip, 2 3/16- x 36-inch (1- x 91-cm.) wood dowels, 1/4 x 36-inch dowel, block plane, 3/16-inch and 1/4-inch drill bits, saw, wood/craft glue, plaster of

Paris, plastic pot that fits inside your display pot, green paint, brush, dyed green pampas grass, green spool wire

## Instructions

To assemble the tree, dowel rods are inserted through holes in the wood strip at alternating right angles spaced 4 inches (10 cm.) apart on center. To do this, measure 4 inches down from the top of the wood strip and mark the center. Make 2 more marks on the wood in 8-inch (20-cm.) increments and drill these 3 holes with a 3/16-inch bit. On the other side of the wood strip, make and drill 3 holes at 8-inch intervals, using a 3/16-inch drill bit for the

first 2 holes and a 1/4-inch bit for the last hole. Be sure to drill straight (at 90° to the wood) so that your dowel will end up horizontal. (Note: If your holes aren't straight you can enlarge the hole, wedge the dowel in at the correct angle, and secure in place with glue.) Next, drill a 1/4- x 2-inch deep hole in the bottom of the wood strip.

Using the plane, trim down almost the entire wood strip from the top to 6 inches (15 cm.) up from the base to form a gradual taper that is round and about half an inch at the top. Insert the dowels through the holes, starting with the smallest and working down to the largest. Center the dowels and glue them in position.

Mix the plaster of Paris in the plastic container and insert the wood strip 3 inches (7 cm.) into the center of the plaster, making sure it is straight up and down. Hold in place until the plaster hardens. When the plaster has cooled, insert the 1/4-inch dowel into the hole in the bottom of the wood strip.

Paint the entire tree green and allow to dry completely. Cut the pampas grass into 4-inch lengths and glue them to the tree, beginning at the top and overlapping the grass as you work your way down. If the finished tree is too bushy for your liking, wrap it with green spool wire to get a more tailored look. Last, place the plastic pot inside a pretty container and decorate the tree.

45

When Jo Lydia and Ian decided to move their pottery studio from France to a small mountain community in the States, they packed 18 rooms of antique furniture (some of which dated back to the 1500s) and their pottery kilns into crates and enjoyed a five-day cruise across the Atlantic aboard the Queen Elizabeth II with their four long-haired Dachshunds. The Dachshunds, of course, were the darlings of the cruise!

The warm, cozy atmosphere of their new mountain-top home captures all the romance of their former home in France and the spicy flavor of their time in Spain. Infused with their personalities and their past, the home serves as inspiration for new pottery designs and techniques.

In the dining room, antiques, art, and precious porcelain come together as the perfect backdrop for a memorable holiday meal. We've added just a few touches of greenery, some candle holders, some colorful place mats, and two Victorian-style projects that complement the Cravens' antique lace collection, the kilims, and the beautiful textures in the porcelain.

## Candle Holders
*(on page 47)*

These candle holders look lovely when arranged in small groups on a dining room table and are very inexpensive to make.

### Materials for Each Candle Holder

Wooden craft candle holder, 2 4-inch (10-cm.) terra cotta plant saucers, 5-inch (12-cm.) tall pinecone, 2 1-1/2 inch (4-cm.) wood screws, 2 rubber washers to fit screws, 1/4-inch and 3/16th drill bits, glue gun, gold craft paint, black spray paint, tube of turquoise acrylic paint, walnut stain

### Instructions

Mark and drill a 1/4-inch hole in the center of each saucer. (Support the saucer with wood while you are drilling.) Cut an inch off the pinecone's pointed end and trim the bottom end flush. Drill a 1-inch deep hole in the center of the pinecone at both ends using a 3/16-inch drill bit.

To assemble, place the screw through the wooden candle holder and the saucer and gently screw them into the pinecone, dabbing in a little hot glue as you go. Attach the bottom saucer in the same manner, using the washer between the screw and the saucer.

Spray the candle holder with the black paint. After the black paint has dried, paint the candle holder with watered down turquoise paint and then add gold highlights. Create an antique look by applying a coat of walnut stain and wiping off any excess with a dry, lint-free rag.

### Tip

The most difficult part of this project is drilling a straight hole into the pinecone, so take your time when you line up the drill and don't give up too easily.

## Kilim-Patterned Place Mats

These bright canvas place mats wipe clean after even the messiest holiday spill. Although they look difficult to paint, they are actually quite simple but a little time-consuming.

### Materials

4 pieces of prepared canvas-measuring 14 x 20 inches (36 x 50 cm.), of 1/2-inch (1-1/4-cm.) grid hardware cloth at least as big as the canvas, 1/-2-inch flat-headed paint brush, tubes of acrylic paint in black, cadmium yellow, brilliant orange, ultra marine blue, cadmium red, permanent green deep, glue gun

### Instructions

Thin black paint with water until it's the consistency of syrup and use it to paint a base coat on all of the canvases. Measure and mark a center line through each canvas in both directions to help you keep the hardware cloth square.

Tape the canvas down on a flat surface and then tape the hardware cloth squarely on top of it. Using the pattern on page 144, count off the squares and paint them accordingly. When you've finished painting, turn under a 1-inch (2-1/2-cm.) hem and hot-glue in place.

### Tip

Use colored pencils to indicated the colors with small dots so you don't have to keep referring back to the pattern.

### Tip

Look for small lace forms in your local sewing shop to fill with colorful, fragrant potpourri. If you have a passion for lace, the forms can also be made from antique lace scraps or even made from scratch with Battenberg tape and cotton thread.

## Découpage Under Glass

For those of us who enjoy collecting and displaying plates, these projects are sure to become a favorite.

### Materials

Clear glass plate, small scissors (appliqué or cuticle scissors work best), paper cutouts, a second plate of the same general size as the plate to be decorated, grease pencil or glass marker, thin clear-drying water-based craft glue, background paper or spray paint, 1-inch (2-1/2 cm.) sponge brush, felt, aerosol pearl spray, clear finish sealant (brush-on or spray). Optional materials: liquid acrylic paint, gold metallic marker, rub-on metallic gold paint, small detail brush, thick craft glue for felt

### Instructions

Clean the plate to be decorated with soap and water and allow to dry thoroughly. Look through magazines, greeting cards, and gift wrap papers to find pictures. (The paper can be of different weights.) Cut out the pictures with as much detail as possible.

Arrange the pictures on the second plate until you're happy with their placement. Place the plate to be decorated on top and trace the outline of the positions directly onto the plate with a grease pencil or marker. Remember to note which cutouts lay in the front so you'll know to glue them on first.

Spread an even layer of glue on the front of each cutout with your fingers and place them where the tracings indicate on the back of the plate. Gently smooth out any wrinkles and use a damp cloth to blot the cutouts until any trapped air bubbles are released. If you're using a plate with ridges, be sure the cutouts conform to the shape. Work with only one cutout at a time and be sure to blot away any excess glue on the plate.

Allow all of the cutouts to dry completely, keeping in mind that glossy and foil papers will take longer to dry. Outline all of the cutouts with a gold marker if desired and allow to dry completely.

Create a background design for the plate with paper or spray paint. If you choose to use a paper background, simply spread a thin layer of glue over the back of the plate with a sponge brush and smooth the paper in place, working from the center outward. Use a damp cloth to smooth the edges and remove any excess glue. Finish the background with paper or paint.

You can also create interesting effects with paper doilies or by applying thin coats of pearl spray between the cutouts and the background.

To finish with paper, spread a thin layer of glue over the back of the plate with a sponge brush and place a sheet of medium or lightweight paper that's slightly larger than the plate on top of the glue. Smooth the wrinkles outward from the center. If needed, cut small slits at the edges and allow them to overlap as smoothly as possible. Use a damp cloth to smooth the edges and remove excess glue. Trim the paper evenly along the edge of the plate, making sure all of the edges are securely glued. Allow to dry and then paint the back with liquid acrylic or spray paint. Allow to dry completely and then apply a clear finishing sealer.

To finish with spray paint, first make sure all of the cutout's edges are securely glued down. Then apply thin coats of spray paint until no color from the back of the cutouts shows through. Allow to dry completely and apply a coat of clear sealer.

Cut out a piece of felt to fit the center area where the plate will rest and attach to the back with craft glue. Last, apply a gold border around the plate's edge if desired with metallic paint or a gold marker. Allow the edges to dry completely before displaying.

51

## Victorian Tableau

This intriguing Victorian-style shadow box makes a dramatically different Christmas gift and can be personalized with special Christmas cards, symbolic ornaments, or romantic mementos.

### Materials
12- x 18-inch (30- x 46-cm.) unpainted shadow box frame (available at craft stores), gold spray paint, 14- x 20-inch (36- x 50-cm.) piece of fabric in a solid color (silk moire works well), glass to cover the tableau, masking tape, glue gun, cardboard ornaments, pictures cut from magazines or cards, Christmas craft novelties (small silk wreaths, trees, beads, etc.), silk flowers and greenery, glue gun, photocopied sheet music, cup of brewed coffee

### Instructions
Remove the back of the frame and spray the frame gold on both sides. Cover the right side of the frame's back with the solid fabric, gluing and taping on the back side as needed. Photocopy a sheet of music. (We used a 16th century holiday piece written for wind instruments). Create an aged appearance on the sheet music by first placing the sheet music flat on a cookie sheet, spritzing the paper with water, and then pouring a cup of strong coffee evenly over the paper. Bake the paper in a 200° oven to create a parchment effect.

Roll the sheet music on its diagonal around a pencil. Unroll the music and place it in the center of your fabric-covered board according to the photo. Arrange the craft novelties and fill in any bare spots with the silk flowers and greenery. When you have achieved a pleasing design, begin hot-gluing the various components in position one at a time. When finished, put the glass in the frame, re-fasten the back, and attach a wire to hang.

The unique gentility of this home's architecture and decor make it a beautiful backdrop for holiday decorations of lace, ribbons, and stuffed animals. The home's owner, Candee, fell in love with the house on a family vacation trip, making an offer to purchase before the trip ended, and moving her husband and children across the country on short notice. The beauty and grace of the house perfectly captures the personality of Candee, and the home is also residence to a personable collection of cats, dogs, chickens, and even a goat named Millie.

The room's soft colors provide a beautiful contrast for Christmas greenery. We chose a mixture of eucalyptus, boxwood, and other evergreens whose varying textures keep the eye from becoming bored with one continuous color. Despite a prevalent assumption that red and pastel colors don't work together, we chose dolls dressed in red as accents and were quite happy with the results.

## Satin Ornaments Wreath

Created with dried flowers, elegant ribbon, and satin ribbon, this large bow makes a special pastel Christmas display and serves as a focal point for the two complementary topiaries.

### Materials

22-inch (55-cm.) foam base, Spanish moss, floral pins, 3 yards of 7-inch-wide (17-cm.) wired tapestry ribbon, 6 yards of 4-inch-wide (10-cm.) paper ribbon, 4 yards of 1/4-inch (2/3-cm.) metallic gold ribbon, floral picks, floral wire, dried globe amaranth blooms in pink, peach, and white, satin ball ornaments, dried blue hydrangea, poppy seed heads, eucalyptus pods, dried German statice, gold highlight powder, 4 white silk roses, glue gun, angel ornament

### Instructions

Prepare the base by covering it with a layer of Spanish moss using floral pins. Tie the wired ribbon into a bow, position the bow on the wreath, and wire in place. Form curves and loops in the bow's streamers.

Cut the German statice into 3-inch (7-1/2-cm.) lengths and form mini bouquets of 3 to 5 stems each. Attach the bouquets to floral picks and loosely cover the wreath by inserting the picks into the foam. Position the paper ribbon and hot-glue in place.

Wire and hot-glue the satin balls around the wreath and fill in the remaining spaces with single blooms of globe amaranth and the remaining natural materials. Cut the gold ribbon into pieces of equal length and glue them diagonally over the tops of each ornament. Attach the angel with wire and then add sparkle to the poppy seed pods by applying a little gilding powder.

## Pastel Topiary Duo

These statuesque indoor trees could easily grace a tabletop as well as a mantel. Note how the slender trunk accents the fullness and elegance of the topiary's top.

### Materials for Each Topiary

2-inch (5-cm.) foam ball, 24- x 1/2-inch (46- x 1-1/4-cm.) twig for stem, Spanish moss, floral pins, plaster of Paris, small flower pot, floral foam, dried blue hydrangea, eucalyptus, gilding powder, pomegranates, poppy seed heads, dried German statice, small angel ornament, strong straight stems or sticks 1/4- to 1/8-inch (2/3- to 1/3-cm.) in diameter (yarrow stems work well), 4-inch (10 cm.) paper ribbon

Insert the eucalyptus stems into the foam ball, beginning at the bottom. Gild the poppy seed heads and the pomegranates with the powder. Wire the pomegranates to stems and insert into the foam ball. Insert poppies into the foam also. Fill in the spaces with the remaining natural materials. Wire the ornament to a stem and place in the center front of the arrangement. Tie a bow around the tree trunk and secure with hot glue.

## Instructions

Fill the bottom half (or more if your vase is tall) of the vase with sand for stability. Cut the foam with a serrated knife to fit securely over sand so it rests about an inch lower than the rim of the vase.

Insert the eucalyptus stems one at a time, forming a large, round arrangement. Randomly fill in the arrangement with additional stems of dried materials. Fill in any bare spots by hot-gluing in small pieces of celosia.

Meander the ribbon through the arrangement to echo its shape and add sparkle by rubbing the gilding powder onto the poppy seed heads.

# Floral Fireside Arrangement

This glorious arrangement is even more appealing at eye level and is ideal for dressing up bare corner tables or bookshelves. The materials were chosen to complement the wreath and topiaries.

## Materials

Tall, slender vase, small block of wet florist's foam, sand, glue gun, dried eucalyptus, wild grass, nigella, celosia, pink hydrangea, lilies, gilding powder, poppy seed heads, 3 yards of 1/4-inch (2/3-cm.) metallic gold ribbon

## Instructions

Arrange small pieces of floral foam inside the flower pot (to absorb the plaster as it expands) and fill the pot with plaster of Paris. Position the twig in the center of the pot and allow to dry. Insert the top of the twig about an inch into the foam ball. Remove and fill the hole with hot glue and then insert the stem again. Cover the foam ball with Spanish moss using floral pins.

## Faux Marble Ginger Jar

This unique project combines the pleasant shapes of terra cotta pots (pictured right) with the elegant look of marble to make holiday storage containers. We've used several colors to demonstrate the versatility of this technique. This project is a lot more simple than it looks, but a little messy so you may want to protect your work area.

### Materials

White artist's gesso, terra cotta pots (they can be any size but should fit together well and form a pleasing shape when glued together), oil-based paint (1 tube each in permanent green deep, black, white, raw umber, yellow ocher, cobalt blue, and cadmium red), epoxy cement, bird feathers ranging in size from 4 to 8 inches (10 to 20 cm.), rags, brushes, toothbrush, paper doily, craft glue, 1-1/2-inch (4-cm.) wooden wheel, small gold bead, mineral spirits

### Instructions for White Sicilian Marble

Coat all of the pots with gesso and attach the top pots to each other while the gesso is still wet. Allow the gesso to dry completely. Repeat the above steps with the bottom pots. This will glue the pots together. If you choose to leave them separate to paint, you can use cement to attach them later.

Mix together equal amounts of white and raw umber plus a little yellow ocher and a tiny touch of

black. Thin this mixture with mineral spirits and use a rag to rub a thin coat of this mixture over the white pots to get a milky, off-white color. While the paint is still wet, paint

veins with a #4 brush using grey paint mixed from white and a touch of black. Add a little more black to the grey mixture and use it to run a slightly darker color of paint over the inside of the vein with a fine-pointed brush. The finished vein shape should look like a softened bolt of lightning with branches spreading off the main bolt on both sides. Soften the bolt by dabbing the paint with a clean rag.

### Instructions for Green Marble

Coat all of the pots with gesso and attach the top pots to each other while the gesso is still wet. Allow the gesso to dry completely. Repeat the above steps with the bottom pots.

Paint the pots black with a wide brush. While the paint is still wet, apply broad strokes of green with a large feather. (Mix the green with a little yellow ocher to achieve the right shade.) Dip the toothbrush into the mineral spirits, lightly shake off the excess, and then spatter the mineral spirits over the fresh-painted pots which will open up the paint's surface. Continue spattering until you've covered the entire pot.

Mix together green and white paint until you have a light sage color. Form diagonal lines around the pot with a medium-size feather and then use a small feather to form lines with lightly thinned white paint across the sage lines in the opposite direction to form Xs. Soften the pattern by stroking the pot lightly with a dry, wide, flat brush.

### Instructions for Bottom Saucer of Red Marble

Coat all of the pots with gesso and attach the top pots to each other while the gesso is still wet. Allow the gesso to dry completely. Repeat the above steps with the bottom pots.

Mix together cadmium red and black with a little yellow ocher to form a brick red color. Apply this color as a base coat to the pots with a wide brush. While the paint is still wet, draw widely spaced diagonal lines across the saucer with a feather, and white paint mixed with a little yellow ocher. Soften this pattern by brushing in the opposite diagonal direction with a dry, flat brush.

After the paint has dried completely, go over the marbling veins with cobalt blue to sharpen the veins' edges. When this paint has dried, strengthen the white edges of the veins by going over them again with a finely pointed brush with white paint that's been mixed with a touch of yellow ocher. Decorate your pot with a strip of paper doily that's been painted gold and top off with a large gold bead.

**Tip**
Be sure to start these projects well in advance because they will take at least a week of drying time.

## Poinsettia Serving Tray

This fun project creates a real appreciation for the lovely natural detail of this traditional holiday flower. To paint the tray, transfer the pattern from page 155 onto the tray and paint with the colors indicated, following the basic highlighting and shadowing techniques discussed on page 158. The pattern on the tray matches the lamp shade shown on page 117.

## Gilded Cone Ornaments

These wonderful ornaments were designed by picking up the floral motifs on the fireplace tiles, and you shouldn't feel intimidated by the idea of creating your own designs to complement patterns in your home.

### Materials

Pinecone, glue gun, dried hydrangea, silk flowers, wired ribbon, metallic gold spool wire, craft pearls, aerosol gold paint

### Instructions

Spray the pinecone from all directions with several coats of gold metallic paint. Create a hanger for the ornament by making a 4-inch (10-cm.) loop in a 14-inch (36-cm.) length of gold spool wire. Secure the hanger on the cone by twisting the wire around the inside of the cone several times, and

create spirals in the wire ends by looping them around a pencil.

Make a bow from a length of wired ribbon with figure-eight loops and hot-glue it to the top of the ornament. Then make a regular bow and hot-glue it to the center of the first bow, curving the tendrils down the sides of the cone.

Embellish the ornament with bits of silk flowers, dried hydrangea, and craft pearls, tucking them under the bow and into the pinecone and hot-gluing in place.

## Grapevine Wreath

This wreath uses many of the same design elements as the pinecone to maintain design continuity, but it's not an exact copy.

### Materials

Grapevine wreath base, several lengths of wired craft pearls, glue gun, several stems silk forget-me-nots, narrow pink satin ribbon, opalescent cellophane ribbon, yellow satin ribbon

### Instructions

Weave the cellophane and pink ribbons in and around the vines of the wreath base, securing with hot glue as needed. Make the bow by tying the cellophane and yellow ribbons together, gluing over the places where the cellophane and pink ribbons meet.

Hot-glue the pearls and silk flowers into the wreath, tucking them into position as shown in the photo.

## Fabric Heart Ornament

With just a few scraps of fabric, some old buttons, and a length or two of satin ribbon, you can create ornaments that work well on trees, door knobs, packages, or even hanging on the wall or from the ceiling. The ornament can also be filled with potpourri to make a year 'round lingerie sachet.

### Materials

Tissue paper, gold ribbon, scrap of brocade fabric, narrow satin ribbon, fabric glue, lace, buttons

### Instructions

Trace a heart shape onto a piece of tissue paper and use it as a pattern to cut out two fabric hearts. Pin both ends of a length of gold metallic ribbon on the right side of one of the hearts, and fold the loop down so it will hang on the outside of the heart after it's been sewn.

Pin the hearts right sides together and sew, leaving a 1-inch (2.5-cm.) opening. Turn the heart right sides out, fill with stuffing or potpourri, and sew the opening closed by hand.

Trim with small satin bows, lace, and buttons if desired.

## Angel Pillow

Made with a simple doily (be it old, new, cotton or linen, crochet or lace), this angel pillow fits nicely into the corner of a chair and can remain as a room accent long after Christmas.

### Materials

Large doily, white fabric circle cut slightly smaller than the doily, polyester stuffing, needle, thread, smaller doily for head, fabric circle cut slightly smaller than the head doily, fabric paints or markers for face, silk flowers, ribbons, beads

### Instructions

Hand-stitch the large fabric circle to the back of the large doily, turning under a narrow hem as you go. Fold the doily in half and stitch closed, leaving a small opening. Insert stuffing and hand-sew the doily closed. (Several smaller doilies can be stitched on top for a layered effect if desired.)

Hand-stitch the smaller piece of fabric to the back of the small doily, turning under a narrow hem as you go and leaving a small opening. Stuff and sew opening closed. (You may need to use a second piece of fabric backing to hold the stuffing in place if your doily has large holes.) Stitch the head to the body, create facial features, and decorate around the head by hot-gluing silk flowers and ribbons.

## Angel Doll

The softness of this doll is made doubly sweet with doilies, hankies, tea towels, and eyelet. She's easy to make and precious to snuggle with.

### Materials

12-inch (30-cm.) square of muslin, 6- x 12-inch (15- x 30-cm.) square of white fabric for wings, tea towel or other fabric for dress, cup of tea or coffee for dye, color markers, crayons, polyester stuffing, ribbon, needle, thread, wired star garland, carbon paper

## Instructions

Dye the muslin by dipping it into a cup of tea or coffee, testing on a small corner first to be sure you like the color. When the fabric is dry, iron and fold in half. Place traced or photocopied pattern pieces for head, arms, and legs shown here and on page 150 onto the muslin and pin into position. Cut.

Trace facial features from the pattern onto the fabric with carbon paper. Remove the carbon and re-trace over the features with a per-manent black marker. Color in the hair, eyes, and cheeks with a crayon.

With right sides together, sew the body closed, leaving a small open-ing. Stuff tightly and sew closed. Sew the arms and legs to the body as indicated on the pattern. Fold the wing fabric in half, pin the wing pattern in place, and cut out. Sew right sides together, leaving an opening for stuffing. Clip along edge

of fabric as indicated on pattern. Turn right sides out, stuff, and stitch opening closed.

Fold a tea towel or similar size of fabric in half and stitch the sides closed, leaving an opening wide enough for the doll's arms. Slit the top center open wide enough for the head. Then fold the edges un-der and use a running stitch to gather around the neck of the doll. Form a bow with the ribbon and stitch at the neck. Hand-stitch the wings through the back of the dress into the body. Last, form the halo with a star garland as in-dicated in the drawing and stitch to the back of the doll's head.

Arm · Cut 4

Leg · Cut 4

Body · Cut two

### Tip

Several pattern companies offer a wide variety of craft patterns for small animals such as the bunny shown here. Follow the basic patterns for the animals, and then turn them into Christmas keepsakes by dressing them in clothes made from antique embroidered handkerchiefs, pillowcases, or laces.

### Materials

Thickly-braided raffia base cut to fit your arch, dried German statice, annual statice in pink, purple, and white, yarrow, poppy seed heads, ornamental red peppers, beebalm, pearly everlasting, floral picks, floral tape, glue gun

### Instructions

Trim the German statice into 4-inch (10-cm.) lengths and arrange the stems into small bouquets of 5 stems each. Attach the bouquets to floral picks and wrap each pick with floral tape. Mark the middle point of the braid with a marker

## Palladian Window Garland

A glorious arch of dried flowers reinforces the architectural focal point of this bedroom. The colors of the arch were selected to echo the hues of the upholstery and to promote harmony between the holiday colors of the wall and the drapery fabric. The garland is quite simple to make and well worth the effort considering the expense of having one custom-made.

and begin inserting the picked German statice bouquets into the raffia. (Be sure to alternate sides as you work to ensure uniformity in the finished garland.) When the braid is covered with German statice, arrange the remaining materials around the garland to fill in any bare spots and add color and texture.

**Tip**
To determine the precise length of raffia needed to fit the window, measure the horizontal distance across the window. Divide this number in half, multiply by 3.147, and add 3 inches to each side for overhang. Example: If your window's width is 42 inches, you'd divide this number in half to get 21 inches. Then multiply 21 x 3.147 to get 66 and add 6 inches for the overhang amount to determine you'd need 72 inches of raffia braid.

A tree in the entranceway is a wonderful way to welcome guests. This tree's Victorian-style ribbon and lace decorations were kept simple to highlight their elegance.

## Victorian Lace Fan Ornaments

These lace ornaments are so quick and inexpensive that you could make enough to decorate a large

tree in a single afternoon for just a few dollars.

### Materials

3-inch (7-1/2 cm.) wide lace cut in 10-inch (25-cm.) lengths, thin-gauge floral wire, narrow ribbon, small dried flowers, glue gun

### Instructions

Gather the lace across the bottom until it forms a fan shape and secure by wrapping several times with floral wire. Place the flower stems against the bottom of the fan and attach by wrapping several times with floral wire. Cover the floral wire by hot-gluing a small bow on top of the stems.

## Victorian Potpourri Handkerchiefs

These small Victorian whimsies emit a lovely Christmas fragrance because they've been filled with potpourri. It's a nice idea to keep a large bowl or basket of them near your tree to give as gifts for surprise guests and visiting friends.

### Materials

Antique linen handkerchief (small doilies can be substituted), narrow satin ribbon, potpourri of your choice, dried flowers (optional)

### Instructions

Lay the handkerchief flat on a table, right side up. Place a cup of potpourri in the middle, bring the sides up, and tie with a pretty ribbon.

Tip: A few stems of dried flowers can be tied in with the ribbon as an extra touch.

## Lace and Brocade Heart Pillow

This small pillow is the perfect place to use those pretty bits of lace and buttons you've been saving for years.

### Materials

Brocade fabric, lace, buttons, polyester stuffing

### Instructions

Cut out the pillow and ruffle using the pattern and directions on page 150. Hem one edge of the ruffle and gather the other edge with a basting stitch. Decorate the front of the pillow with buttons, lace, and other scraps you find appealing.

Place both heart pieces right sides together and sew, easing in the ruffle. Leave a small opening on one edge. Fill with stuffing and sew the opening closed by hand. Stitch the ruffle ends together.

### Instructions for Garland

Drape the garland over the doorway, attaching as needed with
small nails. Secure the garland to
the nail heads with wire. Arrange
small bouquets of baby's breath
and wire them into the garland,
starting at the center top and
spacing them in a random but
even fashion.

Millie the goat, pictured above,
is caught admiring the outdoor
decorations. (She's really sizing
them up for an afternoon snack!)
The decorations were created with
simple velvet bows, an evergreen
garland, and hurricane lamps.

## Door Garland and Wreaths

Apples and pink pepper berries
make the perfect Christmas complement to this entryway. If the
weather cooperates, the apples will
stay fresh-looking through the holiday season, although they can be
easily replaced if necessary.

### Materials for Garland

Purchased Fraser fir garland, dried
baby's breath, fresh apples, pink
pepper berries, floral wire, small
nails, floral picks, glue gun

Insert a floral pick into the center core of each apple. Wire the apples by their picks into the garland, starting at the top center and working out from there. Last, add more color by hot-gluing short stems of pepper berries in place.

### Instructions for Wreaths

Arrange the baby's breath into small bouquets and wire them into the wreaths, taking care to position them all at the same angle. Insert a floral pick into the center core of each apple and then wire the apples into the wreaths by their picks. Last, add more color by hot-gluing short stems of pepper berries in place.

## Antique Lace Tablecloth

This small circular table in the dining area becomes a lovely focal point when decorated with a tablecloth made with the lace of family wedding gowns.

### Materials

English net, antique lace (can be scraps from a collection, from old, discarded clothing, or found in second-hand shops), non-stretching string, needle, thread, pins, large sheet of paper, beads and sequins (optional)

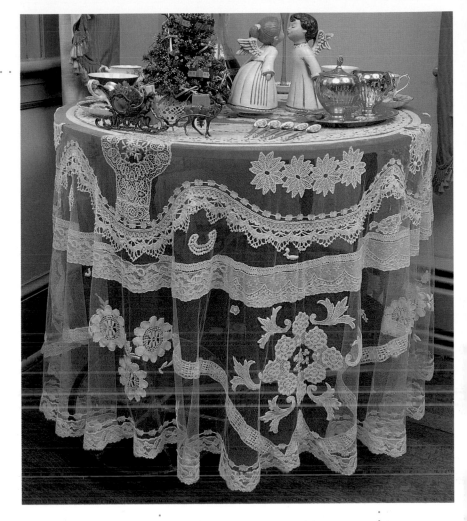

### Instructions

Measure the distance from the floor to across the table and back down to the floor and add 2 inches (5 cm.) for a hem. To make the pattern, divide the measurement in half and draw a straight line that length on the paper's edge. Attach a piece of string to a push pin through the paper and into a protected surface. Tie a pencil to the other end of the string. Starting at the edge of the paper, draw a semi-circular line approximately 1/8 the diameter of the circle.

Fold the fabric in half lengthwise then again widthwise. Then fold the fabric diagonally, holding it at the top center fold. Pin the pattern to the folded fabric, placing the pattern's straight line against the fold line of the fabric. Cut along the semi-circular line. Remove pattern, lay out the net, and hem. Pin the lace pieces in position. Hand sew the lace and add beads and sequins if desired.

### Tip

If you can't find net fabric wide enough to fit the table, you can piece it and cover the seam with lace.

Since this kitchen opens to the main dining and entertainment areas, it plays an important role in setting the mood for a holiday party. The Christmas party menu, tastefully complemented with home-grown herbs, was wonderfully riddled with richness and unique flavors. The culinary presentations provided a focal point and set the tone for the decorating theme. You don't have to be a culinary genius to achieve the same results. Just think of the food as you would an armful of fresh flowers, as something to arrange and decorate with.

The center butcher block table provided the perfect staging area for preparation and presentation of fruits and desserts that would later be moved to the main dining area, and gave guests a glimpse of the treats to come. Sugared fruits help create design continuity as well as provide guests with tasty options to the richer, traditional holiday desserts.

The kitchen's open beam ceiling is decorated with thick swags of sugar-coated Fraser fir to form a backdrop for garlands of tempting candy. To enhance this sugar plum effect, opalescent ice cream cone ornaments were hung from the fir, and the area over the butcher block has been decorated with a small twig tree that was sprayed silver, decorated, and hung upside down to create the effect of a Christmas chandelier.

71

## Candy Garland

A garland of Lifesavers, spice drops, and jelly beans makes a fun pre-party project for children to make and an even better after-party treat. Stringing the candy onto a flexible base of monofilament allows you to drape the garland around cupboards, doorways, and other interesting locations.

### Materials

Embroidery needle, monofilament, several bags of assorted candy

### Instructions

Measure the area where you would like the garland to hang, and cut the monofilament to that length. Thread the needle with the monofilament. Press the needle through the center of each piece of candy and then slide them down the monofilament.

### Tips

The fresher the candy, the easier it will pass through the needle. Be careful not to hang the garland near heat sources such as Christmas tree lights because the candy will melt.

## Ice Cream Cone Ornaments

These wonderful confection ornaments look as delicious hung from a garland as they do on a tree, and a layer of opalescent paint makes them sparkle like magic.

**Materials**

Sugar cones, 4-inch (10-cm.) foam balls, gold thread, opalescent fabric paint, paint brush, glue gun, assorted nuts and dried flowers, plastic craft jewels

**Instructions**

Cut one 12-inch (30-cm.) length of gold thread for each ornament and hot-glue one end to each side of the top of a cone. Brush on a layer of opalescent fabric paint onto each cone and allow to dry completely.

Hot-glue a foam ball inside each cone and hot-glue the nuts onto the ball. Then hot-glue several dried flower blooms and jewels into the nuts and add sparkle by brushing on another layer of opalescent paint over the top of the ornament.

## Gingerbread Stocking

A fun alternative to the traditional Christmas gingerbread house, this stocking can be eaten as a party treat or mounted on a piece of foam, framed, and hung on the wall as a holiday decoration.

**Materials**

Double batch of gingerbread dough, honey, pastry brush, tube of green cake decorating frosting, assorted candy

**Instructions**

Prepare a double batch of gingerbread dough as directed in your favorite recipe. Roll out the dough on a floured surface to a thickness of 1/4-inch (2.3-cm.).

Trace a stocking shape onto a piece of paper, cut it out, and then use it as a pattern for cutting out the gingerbread. Cut the remaining dough into half-inch-wide (1-1/4-cm.) strips.

Position the strips on top of the gingerbread stocking to create a lattice effect, brushing a layer of honey on the back of each strip to secure the two layers together. Bake as directed and decorate with frosting and candy after it cools.

## Beads and Angels Swag

The angel theme for this room was chosen because of an antiqued angel that decorates the bookshelf year 'round, so we honored him with a special place in the mantel's greenery and decorations.

### Materials
Artificial garland of greenery, stems of fresh-cut boxwood or other favorite greenery, floral wire, purchased gold cord and bead braid, ornaments

### Instructions
Position the artificial garland on

the mantel, working to achieve a symmetrical effect and securing with nails or push pins. Weave the stems of fresh boxwood into the garland and secure with wire as needed. Wrap the gold braid around the fresh and artificial greenery, draping to create a fuller look. Position the ornaments as desired and wire in place.

## Garden Centerpiece

A garden pedestal and your favorite greenery helps bring your garden indoors for the holidays. Although the size of this arrangement would probably be overwhelming during another time of the year, it's just right for Christmas.

### Materials
Garden pedestal, block of foam cut to 3x5x5 inches (7x12x12 cm.), adhesive tape, Spanish moss, floral pins, dried pomegranates, eucalyptus, poppy seed heads, globe amaranth, hydrangea, roses, gold craft powder, floral wire, floral tape, glue gun

### Instructions
Tape the foam to the top of the pedestal and use floral pins to cover it with moss. Prepare the materials by wiring the stems of the pomegranates and poppy seed heads, and then gild them by rubbing on a light layer of gold craft powder. Also highlight several of the eucalyptus leaves with the gilding powder.

Insert the stems of the pomegranates, poppy seed heads, and eucalyptus into the foam, and hot-glue in the roses, globe amaranth, and hydrangea.

### Tip
A nice houseplant works just as well as a base: just stick the wired flowers into the plant's dirt.

## Ribbon and Star Garland

Small angel ornaments provide continuity for the room's angel theme, while the gold stars and peach ribbon pick up the colors in the mantel's decorations.

### Materials
Several lengths of wired mylar stars

(available in craft stores), paper ribbon, angel ornaments

### Instructions

Wire the stars onto the staircase or a large piece of furniture, letting them dangle naturally. Tie the paper ribbon at the top end of the staircase and weave it down and around through the stars. Finish by adding the ornaments.

## Basil Pesto Chips

These scrumptious morsels make great cocktail party fanfare—lots of flavor and texture yet not too spicy.

### Ingredients

3 tablespoons (28 g.) fresh basil leaves, finely chopped, or 4 tablespoons (38 g.) dried leaves

1/2 cup (70 g.) flour

1 cup (140 g.) cornmeal

6 tablespoons (90 ml.) basil pesto, purchased or prepared*

1 teaspoon (3 g.) garlic, finely minced

1/2 pound (225 g.) sharp white cheddar cheese, cut in chunks

2 teaspoons (6 g.) powdered blackened redfish spice (equal amounts of paprika, salt, onion powder, garlic powder, cayenne pepper, and lemon pepper)

1/4 teaspoon (3/4 g.) white pepper

1/4 pound (115 g.) cold butter, cut in pieces

2 teaspoons (10 ml.) Pick-A-Pepper sauce (poivrade sauce)

### Instructions

Fine-chop the cheese with a food processor. Add the pesto and basil leaves and process briefly. Add pepper and garlic. Mix together the cornmeal and flour and then add it to the processor with the butter. Continue processing until a ball forms.

Divide the ball into 6 sections. On a well-floured surface, roll each section into a log shape. Wrap in wax paper and chill for at least an hour. Pre-heat oven to 325° (325°C). Cut log rolls into 1/8-inch (1/3-cm.) slices and bake on a cookie sheet for 7 minutes or until golden brown.

### Tip

Make several logs ahead and store them in the freezer, ready to remove, slice, and bake when unexpected company arrives.

## *Basic Basil Pesto

### Ingredients

4 cups (230 g.) of basil leaves, washed and dried

1/4 cup (38 g.) pine nuts, lightly toasted

3 garlic cloves

1/4 cup (60 g.) parmesan cheese, freshly grated

1/2 cup (125 ml.) extra virgin olive oil

### Instructions

Process half the leaves in a food processor to a coarse chop. Add the remainder of the leaves, the garlic, and the pine nuts, and process until finely chopped. While the processor is running, slowly pour in the olive oil and cheese. Yields 1 cup.

## Herbed Montrachet Balls

These goat cheese balls make great holiday snacks or party starters.

### Ingredients

8 ounces (225 g.) Montrachet cheese
1 tablespoon (15 ml.) whipping cream
1/4 cup (38 g.) pecans, finely chopped
2 tablespoons (19 g.) fresh rosemary, finely chopped
2 tablespoons (19 g.) fresh thyme, finely chopped
2 tablespoons (19 g.) fresh parsley, finely chopped

### Instructions

Mix the cream and cheese together until well blended. Roll into small, bite-sized balls. Mix together pecans and herbs, and roll cheese balls in this mixture. Chill at least 2 hours before serving.

## Pecans a la Heather

These tasty tidbits are sure to disappear almost as quickly as you make them.

### Ingredients

3 cups (460 g.) pecan halves
2 teaspoons (10 ml.) water
1 egg white
1/2 cup (100 g.) sugar
1 teaspoon (3 g.) cinnamon
3/4 teaspoon (2 g.) salt
1/2 (1-1/2 g.) teaspoon nutmeg
1/4 teaspoon (3/4 g.) ground cloves
1 tablespoon (15 g.) butter

### Instructions

Beat the water and egg white until foamy and toss it with the pecans. Mix together the sugar, cinnamon, salt, nutmeg, and cloves, and stir into the pecans. Spread a single layer of pecans on a heavily buttered cookie sheet. Bake for 30 minutes in a 300° (300° C) oven, turning once halfway through.

## Weaverville Milling's Baked Brie with Apricots en Croute

Be sure to get your share of this wonderful pastry when it's first served because it won't last long!

### Ingredients

1 package puff pastry sheets
Small brie wheels
Dried apricots, chopped
1 egg white, beaten
Water

### Instructions

Place a single puff pastry sheet in the bottom of a shallow baking pan. Cut the brie wheels to fit together snugly in the center of the sheet, leaving 2 inches (5 cm.) of pastry all around. Sprinkle the apricots over the brie and cover with a top sheet of pastry. Crimp the sides using water. Brush with the beaten egg white and bake for 30 minutes at 350° (180° C) until golden and puffed. Note: The pastry puffs nicer when cooked in a convection oven.

## Christmas Basil and Pesto Torte

Lovely during the holidays, this torte also makes a flavorful treat for garden club meetings or special dinners.

### Ingredients

8 ounces (225 g.) cream cheese, softened
3/4 cup (188 ml.) basil pesto, purchased or prepared, recipe on page 75
1/4 pound (115 g.) butter
4 ounces (115 g.) blue cheese
8 ounces (225 g.) Provolone cheese, thinly sliced
1/2 cup (86 g.) pine nuts
1 large roasted red bell pepper, skinned and cut into strips
1 small jar of sun dried tomatoes
Basil leaves for garnish

### Instructions

Blend together the cream cheese, pesto, butter, and blue cheese in the bowl of a food processor. Line a 5-x9-inch (12-x22-cm.) loaf pan with plastic wrap. Place a layer of provolone cheese on the bottom of the pan, allowing the slices to run a short way up the sides of the pan.

Spread 1/3 of the pesto mixture on top of the cheese and sprinkle with 1/3 of the nuts. Place 1/3 of the tomatoes down the center and add the pepper strips on both sides of the tomatoes. Repeat the procedure for the next two layers. When done layering, fold the plastic wrap up and tightly over the top. Place a brick or other heavy item over the wrapped loaf and refrigerate for several hours. Slice while cold and serve with croutons made from a loaf of French bread brushed with olive oil and baked in a 350° (180° C) oven until golden.

## Smoked Trout Mousse

Served on top of fresh cucumber slices or a crusty piece of French bread, this mousse is a real crowd pleaser.

### Ingredients

1/2 cup (115 g.) Ricotta cheese
4 ounces (115 g.) cream cheese, softened
1 tablespoon (15 ml.) fresh lemon juice
1 tablespoon (9 g.) fresh dill, chopped
Salt and pepper to taste
1 cup (200 g.) smoked trout, flaked
2 tablespoons (18 g.) green onions (spring onions), chopped
1/2 pint (1/4 L.) whipping cream

### Instructions

Blend the ricotta and cream cheese together in a food processor. Add the lemon juice, dill, salt and pepper, and process. Whip cream until fluffy. Fold ricotta and cream cheese mixture into the whipped cream, and add the green onions and smoked trout.

# Mexican Dip

This is where the conversation is sure to take place at your next party. You can bet the talk will be interesting, as everyone will want an excuse and several chances to taste this popular appetizer.

### Ingredients

1 16-ounce (450 g.) can of refried beans (frijoles refritos)
1-1/2 cups (375 ml.) guacamole, purchased or prepared*
1-1/2 cups (375 ml.) sour cream
1 clove garlic, finely minced
1/4 teaspoon (3/4 g.) chilli powder
1/4 teaspoon (3/4 g.) ground cumin
Salt and pepper to taste
1/2 cup (115 g.) sharp cheddar cheese, grated
1/2 cup (115 g.) Muenster cheese, grated
1/2 cup (75 g.) tomatoes, seeded, drained, and finely chopped
1/4 cup (37 g.) black olives, sliced
2 scallions (spring onions), sliced

### Instructions

Spread the beans on the bottom of a glass baking dish and spread the guacamole on top of the beans. Mix together the sour cream, garlic, chili powder, cumin, salt and pepper, and spread this mixture over the guacamole.

Sprinkle on the cheeses and top with the olives, green onions, and tomatoes. Bake at 425° (220° C) for 15 minutes and serve with taco chips.

## *Guacamole

### Ingredients

1 ripened avocado (alligator pear)
Juice of 1/2 lime or 1 tablespoon (15 ml.) juice
2 cloves garlic, finely chopped
1 small tomato, seeded, juiced, and finely chopped
1/2 small onion, finely diced
2 tablespoons (30 ml.) salsa
Salt and pepper to taste

### Instructions

Mash the avocado well and then stir in the remaining ingredients.

# Honey Salad Dressing

This flavorful dressing can be made in advance and used to fill culinary gift baskets.

### Ingredients

1/2 cup (75 g.) onions, finely diced
1 cup (250 ml.) vegetable oil
1/2 cup (125 ml.) vinegar
3/4 (188 ml.) cup ketchup
1/4 cup (63 ml.) honey
1 tablespoon (15 ml.) worcestershire sauce
1 tablespoon (15 ml.) garlic salt
Tabasco (poivrade sauce) to taste

### Instructions

Mix all ingredients together. Keeps well for weeks in refrigerator.

# Dick's Herb Butters

Nothing tops off a loaf of homemade bread better than a thick layer of herb butter. These recipes can easily be made in bulk and used for holiday hostess gifts.

### Ingredients, Basil Butter

1 stick (115 g.) butter, softened
3 cloves garlic, minced
5 tablespoons (47 g.) basil leaves, chopped medium
1 teaspoon (5 ml.) lemon juice
Pepper sauce to taste

### Ingredients, Chive Butter

1 stick (115 g.) butter, softened
1 tablespoon (15 ml.) lime juice
6 tablespoons (57 g.) chives, chopped
1 small anchovy filet
Black pepper to taste

### Instructions

Mix all ingredients in a food processor. Store butter in small jars in the refrigerator or freezer.

## Gourmet Garden's Best Herbal Hash

True comfort food, this hash makes a wonderful winter meal when served with crusty French bread. The list of ingredients is long but the hash is worth the work, and the leftovers freeze well.

### Ingredients

1 3-pound (1350 g.) beef brisket
2 small onions
2 bay leaves
4 whole cloves
1/2 teaspoon (2-1/2 g.) whole black peppercorns
1 pound (450 g.) boiling potatoes
1 pound (450 g.) rutabaga
1 pound (450 g.) carrots
12 ounces (345 g.) thick sliced bacon, diced to 1/2-inch (1-1/4-cm.)
2 large onions, diced
4 cloves of garlic, minced
4 ounces (115 g.) of butter
1-1/2 teaspoons (7 g.) of salt
2 teaspoons (9 g.) light brown sugar, firmly packed
2 teaspoons (6 g.) fresh/dried thyme, chopped
1 teaspoon (3 g.) fresh/dried oregano, chopped
Pinch of nutmeg, freshly grated
1/2 cup (70 g.) fresh parsley, chopped
1 teaspoon (3 g.) fresh/dried rosemary, crumbled
1/2 teaspoon (3/4 g.) sage, crushed
4 teaspoons (30 g.) all-purpose flour
1/2 cup (125 ml.) beer
Fresh-ground pepper to taste
2/3 cup (166 ml.) whipping cream

### Instructions

Cover the brisket, onion, bay leaves, peppercorns, and cloves with water and bring to a boil. Reduce heat and simmer until tender, about 2-1/2 hours. Cool and cut into 1-inch (2-1/2-cm.) cubes. Reserve liquid. Peel the rutabaga, cut it in half, and cook it in the reserved liquid until tender. Remove, cool, and cut into 1-inch cubes.

Peel and cube potatoes and carrots. Cook them in the reserved liquid until tender and again save the liquid. Fry the diced bacon until it starts to crisp in a large skillet; add the onion and cook 5 more minutes. Add the garlic and cook an additional 2 minutes. Add the cooked vegetables and half the butter and cook for 10 minutes over medium high heat, stirring as needed. Sprinkle on salt, sugar, thyme, oregano, nutmeg, rosemary, parsley, and sage. Dust with flour and cook 3 minutes more. Stir in the beer and 1/3 cup of the reserved liquid. Stir often and cook for about 5 minutes until mixture has thickened.

In a flame-proof casserole dish approximately 10x13 inches (25x33 cm.), add the diced brisket and the remaining butter. Cook and stir over medium heat about 10 minutes to brown the beef. Stir in the vegetable mixture and the cream. Season with salt and pepper, and bake in a 375° (190° C) oven for 40 minutes until the top is crusty.

## Seafarer's Quiche

This rich quiche is a favorite of seafood lovers.

### Ingredients

1/2 pound (225 g.) large shrimp (prawns), cooked, peeled, and deveined
1/4 pound (112 g.) crab meat
1 deep dish pie crust
1 egg white, slightly beaten
1 cup (250 ml.) half and half cream (single cream)
2 eggs
1/4 cup (60 g.) Monterey Jack cheese, shredded
1/4 cup (38 g.) fresh parsley, chopped
1 small onion, diced
1 clove of garlic, fincly minced
1 tablespoon (15 g.) butter
Salt and pepper to taste

### Instructions

Pre-heat oven to 375° (190° C). Prick the bottom and sides of the crust with a fork. Line with foil and bake for 10 minutes. Remove the foil and bake for another 6 minutes. Remove the crust from the oven, brush with the beaten egg white, and bake 3 minutes more. Set aside to cool.

Reduce the oven temperature to 350° (180° C). Saute the onion until soft and allow it to cool. In a medium-sized bowl, whisk together the half and half, eggs, parsley, salt, pepper, garlic, and onions. Slice the shrimp in half and cut the crab into small chunks. Place the seafood in the bottom of the pie shell, saving 6 shrimp halves for a garnish. Sprinkle shredded cheese over the seafood and then pour the mixture over the top. Bake 25 minutes or until set.

## Christmas Quiche

Red and green peppers create a festive look while adding a robust flavor.

### Ingredients

Red and green peppers, roasted and chopped
1 deep dish pie crust
1 egg white, slightly beaten
1 cup (250 ml.) milk
2 eggs
1 small onion, diced
1 tablespoon (15 ml.) corn starch (corn flour)
Salt and pepper to taste
1/4 cup (60 g.) sharp white cheddar, shredded

### Instructions

Pre-heat oven to 375° (190° C). Prick the bottom and sides of the crust with a fork. Line with foil and bake for 10 minutes. Remove the foil and bake for another 6 minutes. Remove the crust from the oven, brush with the beaten egg white, and bake 3 minutes more. Set aside to cool. Reduce the oven temperature to 350° (180° C).

In a medium-sized bowl, whisk together the eggs, milk, onion, corn starch, salt, and pepper. Drain the peppers well and arrange them on the bottom of the crust, saving a few pieces for a garnish. Sprinkle cheese over the peppers and then pour the mixture on top.
Bake 25 minutes or until set.

## Glazed Chocolate Soufflé

Chocolate and raspberries make for a luscious combination in this decadent dessert.

### Ingredients for Cake

2-1/2 sticks (285 g.) butter
1 pound (450 g.) semi-sweet chocolate (dark chocolate)

3 tablespoons (45 ml.) brandy
2 tablespoons (14 g.) almonds, ground
2 tablespoons (17 g.) flour
8 eggs, separated
1/8 teaspoon (3/4 g.) salt
16 tablespoons (240 g.) sugar

### Ingredients for Filling

1/2 cup (125 ml.) seedless raspberry preserves
1 tablespoon (9 g.) spearmint leaves, finely chopped or crumbled (optional)

### Ingredients for Glaze

1-1/2 sticks (175 g.) butter
4 ounces (112 g.) semi-sweet chocolate (dark chocolate)
4 ounces (112 g.) German sweet chocolate (light chocolate)
6 tablespoons (90 ml.) light corn syrup (golden syrup)
4 tablespoons (60 ml.) water
2 tablespoons (30 ml.) brandy
2 tablespoons (30 ml.) raspberry liqueur/Kirsch

### Instructions for Cake

Combine the butter, chocolate, and brandy, and melt over a double boiler. Stir in the flour, almonds, and 8 tablespoons of sugar. Beat the egg yolks and salt until they're thick and a light lemon color, and fold them into the cooled chocolate mixture. Beat the egg whites until soft peaks form and add remaining sugar 1 tablespoon at a time. Fold the egg white mixture into the chocolate mixture and blend well.

Preheat oven to 400° (205° C). Divide the batter between 2 buttered and floured 8-inch (20-cm.) cake pans. Place in the oven and turn heat down to 350° (180° C) and bake 35 minutes. Allow to cool and then chill well before removing from pans to a rack.

Stir the raspberry preserves and the mint together. Place the cake on a rack and spread the raspberry mixture between the layers.

### Instructions for Glaze

Mix all ingredients together in a double boiler until just melted. Allow to cool. Drizzle the glaze over the cake while still on the rack, chill, and then move to a serving plate.

# Christmas Gateau

This three-layer almond sponge cake is light and flavorful with just the right amount of richness for holiday celebrations.

### Ingredients for Cake

6 eggs, separated
3 tablespoons (45 ml.) water
3/4 cup (150 g.) sugar
1 lemon rind, grated
1-1/2 cups (172 g.) almonds, finely ground
1 cup (140 g.) flour
1 teaspoon (3 g.) baking powder
Powdered sugar
Baking parchment

### Ingredients for Frosting

1 cup (200 g.) sugar
3/4 cup (188 ml.) water
6 egg yolks
2-1/2 sticks (285 g.) butter
1 tablespoon (15 ml.) raspberry liqueur/Kirsch

### Ingredients for Chocolate Filling

4 ounces (112 g.) semi-sweet chocolate (dark chocolate)
2 tablespoons (30 ml.) rum
3/4 cup (188 ml.) whipping cream
3 tablespoons (45 g.) sugar

**Ingredients for Cranberry Filling**

1/4 cup (63 ml.) cranberry jelly

1 envelope unflavored gelatin (gelatine)

3 tablespoons (45 ml.) water

3/4 cup (188 ml.) whipping cream

3 tablespoons (45 g.) sugar

Draw three 8-inch circles on baking parchment paper. (Use a cake pan to trace if necessary.) Turn the parchment circles over and butter and flour the inside of the circle. Place the parchment pieces on cookie sheets.

Beat the egg yolks, water, and lemon rind until light and lemon colored; then gradually beat in the sugar. Sift together flour and baking powder and sift into mixture, stirring constantly. In a separate bowl, beat the egg whites until soft peaks form. Add half the egg whites to the yolk mixture; sprinkle with half of the al monds and fold together. Fold in the remaining egg whites and almonds. Divide the batter into three equal parts and place on the center of each parchment circle. Spread the batter evenly inside the circle. Bake in a 375° (190° C) oven for 10 minutes. Reduce the oven temperature to 350° (180° C) and continue baking for another 8 minutes or until cake springs back lightly and a toothpick comes out of the center clean. Allow to cool 5 minutes. Turn onto a piece of foil that has been dusted with powdered sugar and peel the parchment off. Cover lightly with wax paper and allow to cool completely.

**Instructions for Frosting**

In a saucepan, bring the sugar and water to boil over medium heat, stirring constantly. Allow to boil without stirring until the temperature reaches 280° (135° C) on a candy thermometer. Beat the egg yolks un-

til thick and lemon colored. Add sugar syrup to egg yolks while beating. Continue beating until light and cool. Gradually beat in small pieces of softened butter and then the kirsch.

**Instructions for Chocolate Filling**

Melt the chocolate in a double boiler with the rum and allow to cool. Beat the whipping cream and sugar until stiff. Fold in the chocolate and rum mixture.

**Instructions for Cranberry Jelly**

Melt the cranberry jelly in a saucepan and allow to cool. In a separate pan, dissolve the gelatin in three tablespoons of water over low heat. Whip the cream and sugar until stiff. Fold the cranberry jelly and the gelatin into the whipped cream. Assemble the cake by spreading the chocolate filling over the bottom layer of the cake. Put the next layer in place and spread on the cranberry jelly. Position the top layer and spread on two-thirds of the buttercream frosting. To decorate, place the remaining frosting in a pastry bag with a rosette tip. Decorate around the top of the cake and then sprinkle with preserved fruit bits if desired.

# Pear and Caramel Tart

This sumptuous dessert is the perfect finale for a winter meal. Served hot or cold, its light fruit taste is a welcome treat.

**Ingredients**

8 fresh pears

Juice of 1 large lemon mixed with 1/2 cup (125 ml.) water

1-1/3 cups (265 g.) sugar

1 stick (115 g.) butter, cut in small pieces

1 store-bought deep dish pie crust, defrosted and gently folded into quarters

1 star fruit (carambola)

**Instructions**

Peel and core the pears and then slice them in wedges. Sprinkle the lemon juice and water mixture over the pears and allow to sit for 15 minutes. Drain well and pat dry.

Melt the butter in a 9-inch (22-cm.) cast iron fry pan over medium high heat and stir in the sugar with a wooden spoon. Cook for several minutes until syrupy and caramel colored; then remove from heat.

Arrange the pears in a pinwheel pattern on top of the caramelized sugar in the bottom of the pan. Layer the remaining pear slices to fit tightly together, mounding them up higher in the center.

Return the pan to the heat and cook for 35 minutes, pressing down the pears with a smaller sized pan lid to keep them compressed. Remove from the heat and let cool.

Carefully place the uncooked pie dough on top of the pears and open to a full circle. Press down the crust edges between the pan and the pears. Cut air holes in top of the dough in several places and place the pan in a pre-heated 425° (220° C) oven and cook for 25 minutes or until golden brown.

To serve, place a dish over the pan and flip over. (Remember, the pan will be very hot!) Garnish with star fruit cut in 1/4-inch (2/3-cm.) slices for a holiday look and drizzle any remaining caramel over the star fruit. Serve with whipped cream or ice cream.

## Cascading Ornament Wreath

Decorating the tree with natural materials left the traditional ornaments all dressed up with no place to go, so we designed a wreath to display them.

### Materials
Artificial evergreen wreath, fabric-covered band box, ornaments, tinsel, wire

### Instructions
Fill the bottom of the band box with crumpled newspaper and make a small hole in the back and bottom of the box. Group together bits of tinsel and ornaments and wire them to the box through the hole. Arrange enough additional groupings of tinsel and ornaments to fill the box and wire them in place so they appear to be spilling out. Wire the lid to the back of the box.

Wire the remaining ornaments to the wreath base, spacing them evenly to achieve a full look and leaving a space at the inside bottom of the wreath for the band box. Last, wire the band box securely to the wreath and drape the remaining tinsel around the wreath.

## Fireplace Garland

This garland was designed as a companion to the ornament wreath, with clear glass ornaments and tinsel to suggest bubbles and grass in a fish pond and make the fish look perfectly at home.

### Materials
Enough purchased fresh evergreen garland to drape gracefully across your fireplace or other focal point, ornament hangers, tinsel, ornaments, wired ribbon

### Instructions
Wire the garland into position and then loop the ribbon through the garland. Hang the tinsel and ornaments in the garland.

### Tip
Be sure to keep potential fire hazards in mind when deciding the position and dangling length of the garland and ornaments.

## Natural Tree

This somewhat unusual approach to tree decorating was inspired by floral tapestry designs. Although it's not difficult or time-consuming, it does require a good amount of dried flowers and foliage, but they can always be re-used after the holidays for craft projects.

### Materials
Evergreen tree (we chose a Fraser fir because the needles remain fresh for a long time), tree lights, dried flowers, herbs and grasses, silk flowers, a few ornaments, tree topper

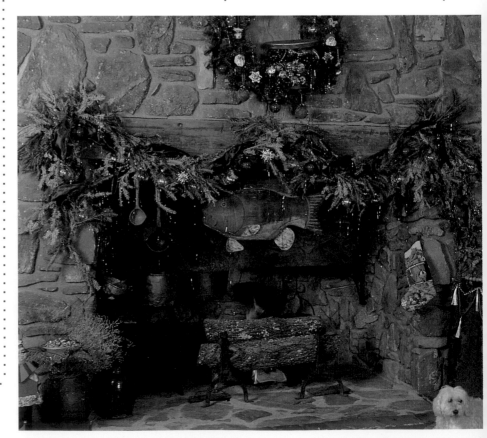

## Instructions

Arrange the lights on the tree and then begin filling in the spaces between the branches with the least favorite of your dried materials, keeping the ends of the materials even with the tips of the branches. Place identical and similar materials evenly around the tree.

Place your best materials last at eye level in the front of the tree. Attach silk flowers and traditional ornaments last.

## Tip

Don't be afraid to try this tree if you don't have a lot of dried materials; just remember to bunch the materials in the front of the tree at eye level to create the best tapestry effect.

The renovation possibilities were both exciting and scary when Paula and Bill Barnes first toured this 1898 bungalow 2 years ago. By the time the first wall was knocked out, though, they knew they'd made the right decision. The challenge, of course, was to maintain as much of the original architectural and design elements from the time period while creating a more practical living area. The renovations included the addition of a large master bedroom suite, a marvelous white tile kitchen, and a life-size Victorian play house complete with plaster walls, windows, and lights.

The projects for the living room were designed to enchant and amuse the Barnes' four young children as well as complement their collection of American antiques. The simple, bright colors create a playful atmosphere, and most of the pro-jects, such as the soft sculpture garland and the stocking wreath, are safe for young children to play with. The quilt makes a wonderful cover for Paula and her 5-year-old to cuddle under for story time, and Paula hopes he'll remember these days in years to come when the quilt has been passed on to him for his own children to enjoy.

# Teddy Bear
# Party Favor

*(on page 85)*

This adorable trinket was made by assembling small craft novelties with hot glue. It makes a special gift to occupy children while the guests talk.

**Materials**

Miniature teddy bear, sleigh, glue gun, plastic apples, rocking horse, narrow ribbon, bow, cotton fabric

**Instructions**

Hot-glue the teddy bear, bow, and rocking horse to the sleigh. Wrap the miniature packages in fabric and decorate with narrow ribbon. Last, arrange the packages and the apples around the sleigh and hot-glue in place.

# 3-Wreath
# Ribbon Garland

A long length of wired ribbon ties this wreath arrangement together. The arrangement is ideal if you have a large wall to cover or if you want to combine wreaths from years past with new ones, and while the wired ribbon is expensive, you should think of it as an investment since it can be re-used every year.

**Materials**

Several yards of 6-inch (15-cm.) wire ribbon, 2 20-inch grapevine wreath bases, 1 16-inch foam base covered with Spanish moss, glue gun, canella berries, assortment of mosses, dried cayenne peppers, strawberry corn, pepper berries, paint brush, liquid glitter

**Instructions for Center Wreath**

Hot-glue the strawberry corn loosely around the wreath base at varying angles. Fill in the holes with short stems of pepper berries and hot peppers and hot-glue in place. Create the sparkling effect by painting the entire surface area of the wreath with liquid glitter.

**Instructions for Outer Wreaths**

Pull off small pieces of the mosses and tuck them into the vine, securing with hot glue as needed. Cut the stems of canella berries to 4-inch (10-cm.) lengths and hot-glue around the wreath.

### Instructions for Assembly

Tie a bow in the center of the ribbon and wire it to the center wreath through its loop, reinforcing with hot glue if needed. Tie a bow on each end of the ribbon and hang.

## Papier-Mâché Angel

Inspired by memorable church mosaics from the designer's childhood, this faux tile angel is actually made from papier-mâché. The project is simple to do but a little time consuming because the mâché takes at least a week to dry.

**Materials**

3-1/2 packages of instant papier-mâché mix, 1 24- x 48- x 1/2-inch (60- x 120- x 1-1/4-cm.) exterior plywood board base, wide roll of plastic wrap, 3 1- x 36-inch (2-1/2- x 90-cm.) dowels, 1 2 x 4 foot piece of 1/2-inch grid hardware cloth, several tubes of acrylic paint, 1/2-inch brush, gold paint pen

**Instructions**

Draw a half circle arc at the top of the plywood base. (See tip.) Mix 1 package of papier-mâché in a large freezer bag according to the directions on the package and use it to apply a layer of mâché onto the base to a thickness of 1/2 inch (1-1/4 cm.) Repeat the process with the remaining packages of mâché until the base is fairly evenly covered.

Cover the mâché with a tight layer of plastic wrap, overlapping at the edges and wrapping behind the base. Place a 1-inch dowel on each side of the board and secure with tape so they don't roll off. Use the third dowel like a rolling pin to create a flat, even surface of mâché, adjusting the plastic if necessary to keep it smooth.

Remove the plastic wrap and carefully place the hardware cloth on top of the mâché. Use the dowel to press the hardware cloth into the mâché deep enough to create a tile effect but not deep enough to submerge the wire. Leave the hardware cloth in place for two hours and then remove.

Allow the mâché to dry. (The average drying time is one week, although drying times vary depending on humidity.) Prime the mâché with a layer of black gesso and paint as directed in the diagram on page 147.

**Tip**

To draw a perfect arc, measure and cut out a piece of cardboard 2 x 26 inches (5 x 65 cm). Secure one end of the cardboard in the center bottom of the base with a push pin. Push the tip of a pencil through the top end of the cardboard, 1 inch in from the edge. Use the pencil

**Instructions**

Sand the ark and animals well, and then coat with a layer of stain. Allow to dry completely. Paint the ark and animals in the colors of your choice, using the highlighting and shading techniques explained in the basic craft instructions section on page 158.

**Instructions**

Trace the pattern from page 143 onto a piece of tissue paper and transfer it to the wood. Cut out the wood and sand all pieces. Then assemble the sleigh as directed on the pattern instructions and nail together. Fill the nail holes with plywood filler.

to draw the arc on the base, starting from the lower left and circling around to the lower right.

# Noah's Ark

Painting the ark and its animals makes a great family project, and the finished product is the perfect decorative accessory for any home. Don't despair if you don't have enough time to finish all the animals: adding new ones to the collection every year is half the fun.

**Materials**

Wooden ark and animals (sold in larger craft stores), sand paper, wood stain, acrylic paints, assortment of flat and round brushes

# Country Sleigh

A sleigh is a wonderful touch for under the Christmas tree, and the classic lines of this one are sure to bring out waves of nostalgia in yourself and guests.

**Materials**

1- x 12-foot (30- x 360-cm.) piece of plywood, tracing paper, sand paper, 6 d penny finish nails, plywood filler, green and red paint, gold paint pencil, stain, glue gun, gold braid

Paint the sled green and allow to dry completely. Then trace the designs onto the sled. Outline the designs with the paint pen and then paint the edges red. Create an aged appearance by sanding the edges to let some of the wood show through. Apply a thin coat of stain and then wipe off immediately with a lint-free rag. Last, tie the gold braid through the holes on either side of the sleigh.

## Tiny Twig Furniture

Made from just a handful of twigs and an enchanted imagination, these tiny furniture pieces are perfect for a miniature room or displayed on tabletops and shelves around your home. In the summer, hide the furniture under large shrubs and trees for the children to discover and invent fairy tales from. The furniture is so simple to construct that even young children can master its creation. The more intricate the furniture, the more

collectible and valuable it will be in years to come.

### Materials

An assortment of small twigs (some straight, some curved), pruning shears, small dried flowers or herbs (miniature rose buds, salvia, lavender, larkspur, mushrooms, and berries all work well), boxwood, raffia, or dried grasses, larger dried leaves for chair backs or layered table tops, glue gun

### Instructions

Spread your twigs out on a flat surface and wait for inspiration to determine your furniture's design. (If none comes, simply begin copying the furniture shown here and deviate as desired.) Secure the twigs together with hot glue and then cover the glue with raffia.

Make furniture for all the rooms of a house and then embellish the individual pieces with roses, a bit of grapevine, or other dried materials. Miniature baskets of flowers look

A wreath of fresh boxwood makes the perfect backdrop for a grouping of twig furniture and colorful, miniature wrapped gifts.

lovely on book shelves and pillow covers can be made by gluing dried leaves and petals onto larger leaves. Seat chairs can be made by weaving small stems of grass. By now you've got the idea and fairy spirit so have fun!

**Tip**
This work is so detailed that it's worth buying a warm melt glue gun if you don't already have one to avoid painful burns.

## Miniature Basket Ornaments

These small baskets are a cinch to make, and they make nice tree ornaments, place settings, or package decorations.

### Materials

Miniature baskets, spray paint, glue gun, fabric, lace, ribbon, miniature craft apples, hemlock cones

### Instructions

Spray paint the baskets in the color of your choice and allow to dry completely. Hot-glue a length of ribbon or fabric to the basket handles and decorate their rims

by hot-gluing lace in place. Fill the inside of the basket with plastic apples (or other miniatures) and hemlock cones and hot-glue in place.

### Materials

Small basket, spray paint, small block of foam, greenery, craft garland, ornaments, glitter pipe cleaners, glue gun

### Instructions

Spray paint the basket and allow to dry completely. Cut a small block of foam to fit inside the basket with a serrated knife. Trim the greenery to 4-inch (10-cm.)

## Country Basket

Made in the same bright country colors as the Christmas chicken, this decorated basket can be filled with hard-boiled eggs dyed yellow for the kids' breakfast and later filled with hot rolls for dinner.

lengths and arrange in and around the basket, securing by inserting into the foam or hot-gluing. Drape the craft garland around the basket and hang small ornaments from the greenery, securing as needed with hot glue. Insert the glitter pipe cleaners into the foam and bend them to create curves.

# Ho Ho Ho! It's Santa Chicken!

The bright country colors of this chicken make it a great centerpiece for a Christmas brunch, and unlike traditional ornate centerpieces, it's childproof.

## Materials

Red felt, 3 different prints of fabric, polyester stuffing, 2 wooden beads (round or oval), 1/4- x 12-inch (2/3- x 30-cm.) wooden dowel, 1- x 2- x 3-inch (2-1/2- x 5- x 7-cm.) wood block, acrylic paints, 2 black beads or buttons, 1 jingle bell, metallic gold thread

## Instructions

Cut out the fabric for all of the pieces except the legs according to the patterns found on page 151. With right sides together, sew each shape together, leaving a small opening. Stuff all of the shapes and then sew all of the openings shut by hand except for the chicken's body. Tack the tree and wings in place by hand and sew on two beads for the eyes.

Cut the dowel into two 6-inch (15-cm.) lengths. Paint the base and wooden beads in the colors of your choice and allow to dry completely. Sharpen the bottom end of the dowels with a pencil sharpener.

Cut out the fabric for the legs, sew, and turn right sides out. Slide the legs over the wooden dowels, leaving 3 inches (7-1/2 cm.) at the top to insert through the beads and into the chicken's body, and 3/4 of an inch (2 cm.) at the bottom for insertion into the block. Secure as needed with a dab of hot glue.

Slide the beads onto the dowel legs and insert them 2 inches into the chicken's body. Hot-glue in place. Drill two holes at an angle in the wood base. Insert the dowels and secure with hot glue.

# Dinner Napkins

Holiday napkins are the perfect touch for a Christmas dinner table, but department store prices can be inhibiting. The thrifty crafter's answer? Buy a yard of holiday fabric, trim into 17- x15-inch (43- x 39-cm.) rectangles, and machine hem.

## Tip

Just a few more minutes' work and another yard of fabric yields a coordinating table runner.

# Miniature Country Living Room Box

From the cookies and milk on the mantel to the tiny wrapped gifts, the charm and allure of this miniature reproduction comes from its fine attention to detail. The miniature can be hung on the wall or displayed on a tabletop, and the room can be a perfect replica of your own home or pure figment from your imagination.

## Materials

Cardboard box, gift wrap in a neutral color, miniature wallpaper (contact paper with a small print can be substituted), assorted pieces and narrow strips of wood, small piece of upholstery fabric, miniature tree, miniature ornaments, assorted miniature furniture, assorted wood cutouts, narrow ribbon, colored wire, felt scraps, model train trestle, wallpaper adhesive, contact cement

## Instructions

Trim the flaps from a cardboard box and wrap the box with gift paper. Wallpaper the walls, ceiling, and floor. (The floor can be hand-pieced with narrow strips of wood instead if desired.) Form the baseboard and ceiling trim with narrow strips of wood and glue in place. Make the rug by fringing a small piece of upholstery fabric. Then form the fireplace with the model train trestle, glue in place, and place the milk and cookies on the mantel. Decorate the tree with

small craft pearls, wood cutouts from a craft store, and with candy canes made from red and white wire twisted together. Make a small skirt for the tree from felt and wrap small pieces of wood in gift paper to form presents. Decorate the remainder of the room with assorted miniature furnishings of your choice.

## Santa's Serving Tray

This fun folk art painting project is fairly simple to cut out and assemble, and makes the perfect place to leave Santa's Christmas Eve treats. We've finished him with an antique look but you can omit the antiquing steps if you'd prefer.

### Materials
1- x 10- x 26-inch (2-1/2- x 25- x 36-cm.) piece of wood for arms, 1- x 13- x 27-inch (2-1/2- x 33- x 67-cm.) piece of wood for body, 2- x 12- x 13-inch (5- x 30- x 33-cm.) piece of wood for base, 1/2- x 8- x 10-inch piece of wood for tray, 1/4- x 1- x 35-inch (2/3- x 2-1/2- x 89-cm.) length of wood stripping, wood glue, wallboard joint compound, putty, folk art paints in assorted colors, garnet paper, screws, provincial stain, 2 bells (optional)

### Instructions
Build the serving tray according to the plans on page 145. Sand all areas with garnet paper until smooth and then vacuum. Draw the features on the face and on the areas to be sculpted with putty. Build up the areas on the hat, beard, and bottom of the shirt with putty and allow to dry 24 hours. Paint all of the puttied areas white. Then paint the face, highlighting areas with dark and light shadows as indicated in the photo. Paint the rest of the serving tray figure and allow the paint to dry.

Create an antiqued look by first sanding some of the wood to make it look worn. Then apply a coat of provincial stain and wipe off any excess with a dry, lint-free rag.

This traditional living room has been dressed up for the holidays in primary reds and greens — colors that appeal especially to young children and to the child hiding in every adult. The crafts feature animals, a Santa, and traditional picture scenes, and are sure to entertain as well as decorate.

## Reginald-the-Reindeer Wreath

A simple wool stocking quickly takes on a personality of its own when it's filled with stuffing and decorated with expressive facial features.

### Materials

2 straw wreath bases in sizes that fit inside each other, wool stocking with the toe and heel in contrasting colors, bag of polyester or cotton stuffing, 3 pieces of 11 x 18 (27 x 46 cm.) red felt, 2 pieces of green felt, 1 small piece of black felt, red yarn, 1- and 3-inch (2-1/2- and 7-1/2 cm.) ribbon, 1 red pompon for nose, pair of plastic craft eyes, wire, fabric glue, glue gun

### Instructions

Place the smaller wreath base inside the larger one and wire the two together. Stuff the stocking compactly and then secure the stuffing in place by pushing in a small square of red felt (cut an inch wider than the stocking's opening). Secure the felt with fabric glue if necessary.

Following the pattern on page 150, cut out the antlers and holly leaves. Position the wire loops in the antlers as shown in the pattern and sew together, leaving a small opening. Stuff tightly, using the eraser end of a pencil if needed to help get stuffing in the corners and curves. Hot-glue the antlers to the head of the dear.

Make the berries by cutting out 4 squares of red felt measuring 4 inches (10 cm.) each. Roll a small piece of polyester filling into a small ball and put it in the center of a piece of felt. Gather up the edges and tie tightly closed with a piece of string or yarn. Trim off excess felt and string.

Working from the right side, force the eyes through the knit of the stocking and hot-glue into position. Cut out the mouth and eyelashes and then glue in place along with the nose (pompon), halter, and wide ribbon. Hold the reindeer against the wreath to position the holly leaves and then hot-glue the holly in place. Last, hot-glue the reindeer and antlers onto the wreath base, and glue the berries in position.

## Teddy's Sweater

Teddy's been good all year and would just be crushed if Santa didn't bring a gift for him. This custom-fit sweater is quick to make and guarantees that Teddy will be well dressed when holiday company drops by.

### Materials

Teddy bear, measuring tape, pair of knitting needles, yarn of your choice

### Instructions

Measure the bear's waistline and add 2 inches (5 cm.). Cast on as many stitches as needed to achieve that measurement. Knit a 1-inch ribbing (K1 P1 for a small bear, K2 P2 for a larger bear) and then continue up in the stockinette stitch until you reach the under arms.

Increase enough stitches to form the sleeve and add a 1-inch rib at the end of the sleeves. The stockinette stitch will curl down at the neck edge so do a few extra rows. Repeat for the back and sew together at shoulders and underarm.

### Tip

Circular knitting needles make the job go much faster.

## Starland Garland

This soft sculpture garland creates a lighter look than traditional greenery garlands and is always a favorite with children.

### Materials

Small pieces of 7 different patterns of fabric, polyester stuffing, 3-inch (7-1/2) ribbon, floral wire

### Instructions

Cut out the stars and wreaths from the patterns on page 151. Make a loop for each shape and sew in place according to pattern. With the right sides together, sew each shape together, leaving a 1-inch opening. Turn right side out.

Stuff the shapes with polyester filling and then hand stitch the opening closed. Thread ribbon through the loops on the back and secure in place with a safety pin or tack with needle and thread. Make two bows and attach them to each end of the ribbon with floral wire as shown in the photo.

## Santa Fireplace Board

The large plywood cut-outs in shapes of snowmen, reindeer, and Santa available in larger craft stores are often purchased to decorate a front lawn, but they also look nice indoors. This Santa stands in front of the fireplace to remind children of all ages to be on their best behavior.

### Materials

Plywood cut-out, acrylic paints, variety of flat and round brushes

### Instructions

Prime and paint the Santa in the colors of your choice with the highlighting and shadowing techniques explained in the basic craft directions on page 158-159.

## Christmas Bird's Home

Too precious to expose to the elements, this birdhouse is just perfect for your coffee table. Try filling the chimney with fragrant cinnamon sticks or with candy canes for the kids to nibble on.

### Materials

1- x 12-inch (2-1/2- x 30-cm.) piece of plywood, wallboard joint compound, 6 "d" penny finish nails, 1/4-inch (2/3-cm.) wide dowel, folk art paint in red, green, and white, piece of scrap 2 x 4 (5 x 10 cm.), sandpaper, putty or textured artists' gesso, wide and narrow paint brushes, stain

### Instructions

Trace the pattern onto the wood and build the house according to the pattern instructions on page 145. Paint the roof red and the house white. To create the appearance of snow, apply putty to the roof and the top of the chimney, working it gently over the sides. Apply light amounts of additional putty around the entrance hole and the bush areas. Allow the putty to dry 24 hours

Paint the putty white and paint the wreath and bushes green. After the wreath paint dries, dab on small dots of red paint to create berries. Allow all paint to dry.

Apply a small amount of white paint to a dry brush and lightly paint around the house to create more snow. Allow the paint to dry completely and then lightly sand the edges of the house. Last, create an aged appearance by applying a thin coat of stain and wiping over it with a dry, lint-free rag.

## Christmas Quilt

This wonderful sampler quilt illustrates how simple it is to create holiday patterns with basic patchwork grids and a variety of holiday fabrics. And while this project will certainly take longer than a weekend to complete, it's well worth the effort when you consider how many yearsz of future enjoyment your family will receive.

### Materials

About 20 small pieces of holiday fabric in solids and prints for patchwork, 3 yards (2.7 m.) of a solid color for background, cotton or polyester batting, fabric for backing

### Instructions

Cut out the patchwork fabric and piece the blocks using the patterns and diagrams on page 152 as a guide. Sew by hand or machine, pressing often as you work. For a wallhanging you'll need 9 blocks; for a twin size bed you'll need 12 blocks; for a full size bed you'll need 16 blocks; and for a queen or king size bed you'll need 20 blocks.

Frame each block with a solid border made from sashes cut to 3 inches (7-1/2 cm.) wide. Assemble the blocks into horizontal rows first and then sew the rows together. Sew on a narrow strip of fabric to form the binding and press the entire quilt well.

Cut a piece of batting and a piece of backing fabric to fit the quilt. (You may need to piece the backing fabric.) Working on a large, flat surface such as the floor, baste all 3 layers together by hand with large stitches. Quilt through all 3 layers using a small running stitch. The quilting stitches can be simple outlines of the patchwork pictures or they can be designs that you trace onto the fabric with a purchased stencil. Finish the edges by folding the binding around the wrong side of the quilt and hemming in place.

101

Since children enjoy Christmas at least as much and probably more than anyone else, it makes sense to spend time decorating their rooms. All of the projects shown here were designed to delight children, and many of them can be made by the children themselves with just a little help from mom or dad.

## Sweatshirt Tree

This adorable felt Christmas tree attaches quickly to a sweatshirt or jacket with safety pins and can be removed when it's laundry time. The tree makes a perfect project for adults to start and children to finish.

### Materials

15- x 20-inch (39- x 50-cm.) piece of green felt, small piece of batting for tree padding, small piece of brown felt, craft glue, narrow trim for tree skirt, small piece of red felt, small piece of narrow ribbon, assorted decorating materials (buttons, appliques, beads, and sequins were used on the tree shown here)

### Instructions

Using the pattern on page 153, cut out 2 tree shapes from the green felt and cut the trunk from the brown felt. Stitch the tree together along the outer edges, ending at the bottom corners of the lower branches. Cut out the padding with the tree pattern and trim off 1/2 inch (1-1/4 cm.) from all of the edges and all of the area below the branches. Insert the padding into the tree.

Stitch along the padding lines to form the branch shapes and stitch along the bottom of the tree. Glue the trunk in place. Decorate the tree as desired, using craft glue to attach the items, and hand-stitch the items in place after the glue has dried. Cut out the tree skirt trim to fit and glue in place. Decorate small squares of red felt with narrow ribbon to create the packages and glue them under the tree. Cut out the stocking and glue in place, and then glue the angel* on top of the tree.

### *Materials for Angel

1-1/2-inch (4-cm.) gathered lace, 6 inches (15 cm.) of narrow ribbon, flesh-colored bead, gold or silver ring, small bell

### *Instructions for Angel

Tightly gather the upper edge of the lace and knot the thread. Sew the bead to the top of the lace and glue the ring to the top of the head to form the halo. Stitch the bell under the skirt and tie the ribbon around the angel's neck, leaving the ends longer than the loops to create the appearance of wings and arms.

# Holiday Animals

Dress up your child's favorite stuffed animals with Christmas outfits made from scraps of holiday fabric and felt. The instructions can easily be adapted so you can custom-fit the clothes to your own animals.

**To Make A Bow-Tie:** Cut a fabric rectangle measuring 15 x 5 inches (39 x 12 cm.). Fold each of the long sides of the rectangle over 1-1/2 inches (4 cm.) and press in place. Now fold each end over 4-1/2 inches (11 cm.) so you have a rect-

angle with no raw edges that measures 6-1/2 x 2 inches (16 x 5 cm.). Fold this rectangle in half lengthwise, wrong sides together, and stitch together 1/4 of an inch (2/3 cm.). Cover the stitching with a small felt or fabric band and attach the bow tie to a stuffed animal with a safety pin.

**To Make A Vest:** Measure the distance around your animal's chest and the distance from the neck to the waist. Cut a rectangle of fur fabric to these measurements. Wrap the rectangle around the animal so the ends meet in the front and secure in place with

straight pins. Use a piece of chalk to outline where the arm holes should be and cut them out. Finish the edges with a narrow edging of fabric cut on the bias.

**To Make A Hat:** Measure the distance around your animal's head and add an inch (2-1/2 cm.). Cut a triangle that is as wide at the base as the measurement and 2 inches (5 cm.) shorter in height. Sew on a narrow fabric border or a quilt batting border on the bottom edge of the triangle. Fold the triangle in half, right sides together, and sew the side seam. Turn right sides out. Hot-glue a small ball of cotton or quilt batting to the top of the hat if desired.

**To Make Additional Accessories:** Some animals, such as the racoon and the dinosaur pictured here, just don't lend themselves to vests or hats, so we've decorated them with a burlap toy bag (stuffed with quilt batting) and a teddy bear print blanket made from a rectangle of fabric with ribbons sewed on the corners. Let your child's imagination do most of the work and have fun!!

# Christmas Laundry Bag

Picking up dirty clothes becomes a joy when the laundry bag looks like Santa's gift bag.

### Materials

1-1/2 yards (1.4 m.) red burlap background fabric, 1/2 yard (.5 m. ) contrasting fabric, 3 small pieces of assorted scrap fabrics, 1/4 yard (.2 m.) teddy bear panel fabric, 1/2 yard adhesive fabric interfacing, white cording, 3 small wooden clothespins

### Instructions

Fold the fabric right sides together and place a pillow in the center. Cut the fabric 2 inches (5 cm.) wider on the sides and 12 (30 cm.) inches longer on the top end than the pillow. Place the pillow aside and sew the side and bottom seams to create the bag. Machine hem the raw edges at the top of the bag. Fold down 6 inches (15 cm.) and press. Pin the folded portion in place and top stitch. Then make a second row of top stitching 1-1/2 inches up from the first row. Separate the threads in the burlap on both sides so there's enough room to insert the cording. Place wrong sides of the contrasting fabric, fabric scraps, and un-cut teddy bear panels on top of the fabric interfacing and iron according to the manufacturer's directions. Using the pattern on page 153, cut out the candy canes and trim out the teddy bear. Peel off the interfacing, position the motifs on the pillow case, and iron.

Measure a length of cording to fit between the candy canes and allow enough extra cording to tie a bow on each end. Attach the cording to the candy canes with a dab of fabric glue or with a needle and thread, and finish by hanging the stockings on the cording with the clothes pins.

## Christmas Tree Skirt

This festive tree skirt makes an ideal covering to hide the base of a small potted evergreen or artificial tree and uses the same motifs as the pillow case and laundry bag. The tree makes an ideal place for kids to assemble gifts they've made themselves for family, friends, and teachers.

### Materials
1 yard (.9 m.) red background fabric, 1/2 yard (.5 m.) contrasting background fabric, 1/2 yard teddy bear panel fabric, 1/2 yard adhesive fabric interfacing

### Instructions
Spread the fabric out in a single thickness on a flat surface. Place a small tea saucer in the center of the fabric and lightly trace its shape onto the fabric. Cut out the circle.

Lightly trace the shape of a larger circle by measuring out 12 inches all the around from the raw edge of the inner circle and cut out. Trace and cut a straight line from the center circle to the edge of the larger circle.

Machine hem both sides of the cut (this will become the back of the tree skirt) and hem the inner circle.

Create the ruffle by cutting a length of contrasting fabric to 100 inches long x 5 inches wide (2-1/2 m x 12 cm.), piecing together if necessary. Fold the strip in half lengthwise with the wrong sides together and press. Fold both short ends under 1/2 inch and machine hem. Make 2 rows of machine gathering stitches on the raw edges. Gather the ruffle to fit the outer edges of the circle, pin in place, and sew together with a top stitch.

Place wrong sides of contrasting fabric and un-cut teddy bear panels on top of the fabric interfacing and iron according to the manufacturer's directions. Using the pattern on page 153, cut out the candy canes and trim out the teddy bear. Peel off the interfacing, position the motifs on the tree skirt, and iron.

## Candy Cane Pillow Case

The teddy bear and candy cane motifs on this bright pillow case encourage sweet dreams in anticipation of Christmas morning.

**Materials**

1-1/2 yards (1.4 m.) red background fabric, 1/4 yard (.2 m.) contrasting fabric, 1/8 yard (.1 m.) teddy bear panel fabric, 1/8 yard adhesive fabric interfacing

**Instructions**

Fold the fabric right sides together and place the pillow in the center. Cut the fabric 2 inches (5 cm.) larger than the pillow. Place the pillow aside and sew the side and bottom seams. Fold the border strip in half (so it's 3 inches, 7-1/2 cm., wide) with wrong sides together and press. Place right sides together and sew side seam. Press raw edges under 1/2 inch (1-1/4 cm.). Position the border over the raw edge of the pillow case so there's a 1-inch (2-1/2 cm.) overlap. Pin in place and top stitch.

Place wrong sides of contrasting fabric and un-cut teddy bear panel on top of the fabric interfacing and iron according to the manufacturer's directions. Using the pattern on page 153, cut out the candy canes and trim out the teddy bear. Peel off the interfacing, position the motifs on the pillow case, and iron.

# Clothes Pin Furniture

This furniture is perfect for small stuffed animals and toys, and it's easy enough for older children to make by themselves or younger children to make with an adult's help.

**Materials**

Clothes pins, wood glue, small scraps of fabric (optional)

**Instructions**

Remove the metal clips from the clothes pins. Arrange them as shown in the photo and secure the pins with glue as you work. (See diagram on page 149.) Add cushions to the furniture if desired with small bits of fabric.

Tip: The furniture shown here makes a good point of reference, but once you've finished a single piece of furniture you have all the skills necessary to begin designing your own.

# Metallic Star Garland

This lovely garland is surprisingly simple to make and can be made in any length.

**Materials**

Box of gold metallic pipe cleaners

**Instructions**

Form the stars by folding the pipe cleaners into accordion pleats in 1-inch (2-1/2 cm.) segments. Open up the pleats, twist the ends together, and you have a star! Form the garland by hooking the star shapes up with circle shapes until the garland is as long as you need.

# Needlework Ornaments

What better way to display your needlework skills than on a tree ornament? The ornaments shown here were made from petit point cross stitch, although they can also be made from larger cross stitch or embroidery patterns.

**Materials**

Needlework canvas, purchased pattern of your choice, floss, cardboard, red felt, chalk pencil, pinking shears, craft glue, red thread

**Instructions**

Block your completed needlework piece and set aside. Decide how big you'd like your completed ornaments to be and look around your home for a circle object that is the same size. (The bottom of a drinking glass often works well.) Trace the circle shape onto cardboard and cut out. Next, trace the circle shape onto the wrong side of the felt and outline the shape with a chalk pencil. Cut out the circle with pinking shears so it is slightly larger than the chalk outline.

## Sheep Ornament
Made from scrap materials, these cuddly sheep ornaments can be made by even young children with just a little cutting help from an adult.

marker to color the face and leg areas of both sides of the sheep. With a black felt tip pen, draw the face and feet and color the edges of the board.

Cut 2 pieces of the fleece from the body pattern, making sure to turn the pattern for the 2nd piece so you will have both sides of the body. To avoid damaging the fur, position the pattern on the wrong side and slide the scissors under the pile when you cut.

Glue the fleece onto the front and back of the cardboard body, adding extra glue along the joined edges. Cut out the ears and tail from the felt and glue them in place, and then tie a bow in the ribbon and glue it under the chin. Last, straighten out the wire in a tree ornament hook and push it into the top of the sheep to form a hanger.

### Materials
White poster board or pad backing, black felt tip pen, tan or light brown marker, small scraps of brown felt, narrow ribbon or cord, 4- x 7-inch (10- x 17-cm.) piece of fake fur, craft glue, craft knife, tree ornament hook

### Instructions
Trace the sheep pattern found on page 153 onto the poster board or cardboard and mark the locations of the eyes, mouth, and nose. Cut out the shapes with a craft knife. Use a brown

Center the needlework design on top of the cardboard circle. Fold the edges over, glue in place, and allow to dry completely. Center the cardboard-backed needlework on top of the red felt and glue in place. Thread a piece of red thread through the red felt at the top of the ornament and tie the ends in a knot several times to make the hanger.

## Teddy Bear Tree Garland

*(on page 107)*

This paper garland makes a great way to entertain the kids on bad weather days. The materials are inexpensive and always available, and it's nice to keep a basket of undecorated garlands under the tree for visiting children to color while the adults chat.

### Materials

Brown paper bag, pencil, scissors, narrow red ribbon, ruler

Using the pattern provided on page 153, trace the teddy bear onto the top layer of the folded paper. Cut out the teddy bears 2 to 4 layers at a time, using the previous layer as a pattern for each new layer. Leave the bears connected at the paws. When you've finished cutting, unfold the bears, decorate them with ribbon, and hang on the tree.

### Materials

Foam egg carton, scraps of felt or yarn in yellow, brown, black, orange, tan, and white, fine-tip markers, uncooked elbow macaroni, scratch paper, craft glue

### Instructions

Cut the felt or yarn scraps into small pieces measuring approximately 1/8 x 3/8 inches (1/3 x 1 cm.) Turn the egg carton upside down and apply glue to the top of each bump to form the scalps. (If you're helping a child with this project, it may be easier to work

### Instructions

Cut the seams of the bag and open it out flat. Cut the longest width of the bag into strips 3 inches (7-1/2 cm.) wide, using a ruler to ensure straight lines. Fold the strips with a fan fold that is 2-1/4 inches (6 cm.) wide and trim off any extra width.

## Egg Carton Christmas Choir

This project was created by a 5-year-old who wanted to get involved with the holiday decorating, and the fun in the project comes from watching the personalities of the choir members evolve. (An older sister helped with decorating the faces.)

with only 1 bump at a time.)

Arrange the felt or yarn pieces in the glue to form the hair and then draw on the faces with the markers. Press 2 pieces of macaroni into each bump to form the arms and secure with glue if needed. Cut the scrap paper into small rectangles and fold in half to form the songbooks. Decorate the songbooks with crayon scribbles and glue them into the macaroni hands.

# Gift Basket Liners

Inexpensive baskets lined with holiday fabrics make the perfect place to assemble small gifts.

## Materials

3/8 yard (.3 m.) Christmas print fabric, 1-1/8 yard (1 m.) of gathered lace or ruffled trim, oblong mushroom basket

## Instructions

Cut 2 rectangles measuring 10-1/2 x 19-1/2 inches (26 x 49 cm.) from the fabric. Place right sides together and sew a half-inch (1-1/4-cm.) seam along one of the long sides. Press seam open. Sew both seams on the shorter sides with the right sides together and press the seams open.

Sew the trim to the long open edge, overlapping and trimming where the ends meet. Press the seam down and top-stitch on the right side of the fabric 1/4-inch (2/3-cm.) from the pressed edge of the fabric. Place the liner in the basket and fill with holiday decorations or goodies.

## Tip

To make the liner reversible, repeat the steps in the first paragraph of instructions with a non-holiday fabric and position the 2 liners with their wrong sides together. Finish the liner as directed in the instructions in the second paragraph.

When people visit Mary and Paul Rifkin, they almost always comment on the warm, pleasant feelings of nostalgia that the Rifkin home evokes. The home is filled with antique toys and early advertising art. The two collections have become so large that they flow from room to room, making the home a virtual toyland for young and old. Paul began collecting when he was in his early 20s, and is always on the lookout for items that once enjoyed a special place in history, such as children's pedal cars from the 30s. The cars became rare because the majority of them were donated to the scrap metal drive during World War II. Paul also collects toys for adults, such as vintage barber shop chairs and a Wurlitzer juke box from the 40s.

Because the Rifkins' home is filled with so many collections, we didn't have to look far for inspiration when it came time to deck their holiday halls. We decided to approach the decorating from a playful point of view and create another collection for them: a collection of stars. We worked with contrasting colors, instead of trying to make everything match or blend, because there was so much going on in the background. The bright red stockings and colorful Southwest star ornaments worked well against the light-colored furnishings and looked right at home with all the toys.

## Sequined and Beaded Stocking

Simple felt pictures decorated with sequins and beads make a special stocking that sparkles and jingles with Christmas excitement.

### Materials

5/8 yard (.6 m.) red velour or felt, 5/8 yard green fabric for lining, white cording, assorted colors of felt scraps, narrow lace, assorted sizes and shapes of sequins, small glass beads and bobbles, buttons, jingle bells

### Instructions

Cut out the red and green stockings and the felt pictures from the patterns here and on page 155.

112

Arrange the motifs on the right side of one of the red stocking pieces and stitch in place. Add detail and sparkle with sequins and beads.

Place the right sides together on both the red and green stockings and sew. Turn each stocking right sides out, fold down the tops 1/2 inch (1-1/4 cm.), and press. Place the green stocking inside of the red stocking and attach them by hand-stitching them to the cording. Allow enough extra cording to form a hanging loop. Last, sew the jingle bells to the bottom of the stocking.

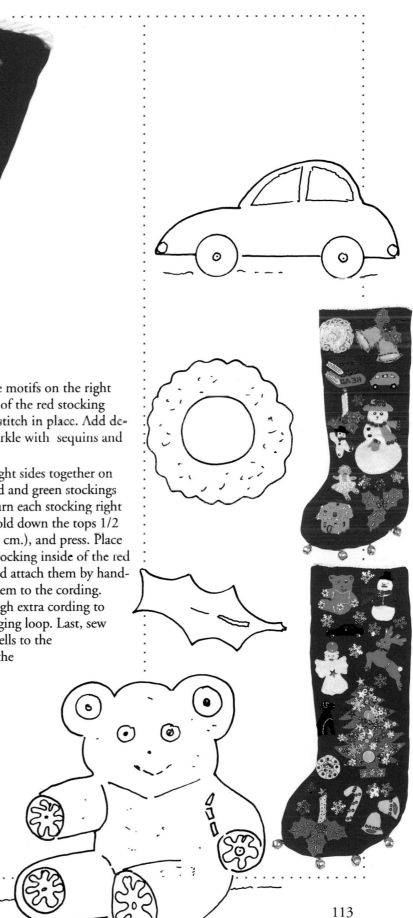

## Christmas Collage

What better way to enjoy personal Christmas mementos than to arrange them in a collage and display the framed design on a wall?

If you're an experienced mat cutter, you can finish the project yourself. If not, we suggest you arrange the items and take your design ideas to a frame shop.

### Materials

4 antique or reproduction ornaments, red beading, 2-inch (5-cm.) craft wreath, silk greenery, large focal point object (an antique game box, special Christmas cards, a magazine cover, a mounted portrait of Santa, an old toy, etc.)

## Poinsettia Lamp Shade

Here's a quick project that creates bright color impact during the day and some lovely light patterns in the evening.

### Materials

Tissue paper, carbon paper, red craft paper large enough to wrap around your lamp shade, craft knife, gold cording, glue gun

### Instructions

Tape a large piece of tissue paper around your lamp shade and tape the overlapping edges in place at the back of the shade. Trace the basic shape of the shade onto the tissue and then draw a straight vertical line from the top to the bottom at the back of the shade.

Remove the tissue and trace the design on page 155 onto the tissue, centering as needed. (For a very large or very small lamp shade you may need to enlarge or reduce the pattern for a better fit.) Transfer the pattern onto the craft paper with carbon paper.

Place the craft paper on a protected surface and cut along the pattern lines with a craft knife. Cut the vertical line on the construction paper, allowing for a 1/2-inch (1-1/4-cm.) overlap. Turn the construction paper right side up and carefully bend back the design edges so the lamp's light will pass through the poinsettia design. Place the craft paper around the lamp shade and carefully glue the back seam together. Last, wrap the gold cording around the top and bottom of the shade and hot-glue in place.

## Jingle Bells

A collection of jingle bells displays well in almost any container. The bells are lovely when they reflect holiday lights and they're fun to pick up and play with. If you don't have enough bells to fill a bowl, try mixing the bells with colored marbles or small pinecones.

### Instructions

Spread out all of your materials on a large piece of tissue paper and play with their arrangement until you're happy with the design. Sketch rough outlines of the objects and their positions and bring the tissue and a copy of this book to a professional framer.

## Southwest Star Ornaments

These ornaments allow you to cover the Christmas tree with bright, colorful stars that coordinate with the rest of the stars in the room.

### Materials

Several sheets of tag board, craft knife, tubes of acrylic paint in burnt umber and other colors of your choice, brushes, textured acrylic snow paint, metallic thread, craft glue, push pins

### Instructions

Cut out, score, and assemble the stars according to the pattern on page 139. Allow the glue to dry completely. Mix the snow-textured paint with small amounts of burnt umber paint until it resembles Southwest stucco and then coat 1 side of each star with this mixture. After the paint has dried, decorate the stars in the patterns pictured here or invent your own. Use the same technique to decorate the other side of the stars.

## Pipe Cleaner Ornaments

These sparkling ornaments can be placed directly on your Christmas tree's branches (instead of hanging with a hook), and they are simple enough for children to make.

### Materials

Package of 12-inch (30-cm.) gold metallic pipe cleaners

### Instructions for Each Ornament

Cut 12 pipe cleaners in half and arrange them in a bundle. Wrap 1 of the pipe cleaners around the middle of the bundles and then bend the other pipe cleaners out from the center to form starbursts.

## Terra Cotta Pot Bells

These colorful bell ornaments coordinate with the Southwest flair of the star ornaments and can be made in a single evening.

**Materials for Each Ornament**

2-inch (5-cm.) terra cotta pot, artist's gesso, acrylic paint, brushes, red metallic pipe cleaners, several jingle bells, glue gun

**Instructions**

Paint the patterns onto the bell with gesso. (We've given you a few patterns on page 154 or you can create your own.) When the gesso has dried completely, paint over it with bright colors of acrylic paint. Thread a metallic pipe cleaner up through the bottom hole of the pot and form a loop in the cleaner. Form 3 pipe cleaners in a bundle and attach them to the top of the pot with the first pipe cleaner. Then wrap the pipe cleaner around the bundle and thread it back through the hole in the pot. Attach the jingle bells to the ends of the pipe cleaner with hot glue.

117

## The Jester's Star Wand Collection

Frivolous and intriguing, these star wands were designed by their jester to revive the wonderful storytelling traditions of the past. To carry on the tradition, have everyone sit in a circle. Have the first person select a wand, stare at it for a moment for inspiration, and then begin telling a story. When they come to a stopping point, pass the wand to the next person. If the next person can not continue the story in an interesting fashion, they must entertain the group with a song, a dance, or a funny joke. This wand game makes a nice ice-breaker for people who rarely see each other except on holidays.

### Materials to Make All the Wands

1 pound of white modeling compound, 2 dowels measuring 3/8 x 18 inches (1 x 46 cm.), 2 dowels measuring 1/4 x 18 inches (2/3 x 46 cm.), acrylic paints in your choice of colors, 1/2- and 1/8-inch (2/3- and 1/3-cm.) jingle bells, red satin cording, plastic craft stars and gem stones, tracing paper, rolling pin, craft knife, butter knife, gold metallic thread, high-shine acrylic spray, gold paint pen, metallic gold paint, brushes

### Instructions for the Blue, Red, and Gold Star Wand

Trace the star pattern on page 139 onto a piece of tissue paper. Form a ball of clay about 2-1/2 inches (6 cm.) in diameter and roll it out to a flat 1/4-inch thickness with a rolling pin. Press a plastic gem star face side down into the surface several times at random to create a star texture. Place the pattern over the clay and cut out the star shape with a craft knife. Remove the pattern. Roll out 1/8- x 8-inch (1/3- x 20-cm.) coils of clay. Using a rolling pin, flatten the coils slightly. Attach the coils to the star, looping and pressing the coil against the side of the star using the edge of a butter knife. When 1 coil ends, simply start another and continue until all of the star has a border. Carefully turn the star face down and place a 3/8-inch dowel rod over the star. (See the pattern on page 139 for reference.) Roll out 2 1/4- x 3-inch (2/3- x 7-cm.) coils of clay and attach them over the dowel rod, pressing the ends into the clay star. Pierce the 5 tips of the star with a cocktail straw so that the gold metallic thread can be attached later.

Make 5 1/4-inch beads and pierce them with the cocktail straw. Bake the star and the beads according to the manufacturer's instructions. When the star has cooled, remove the dowel and decorate it by creating 1/4-inch balls of clay and pressing them onto the dowel 5 inches (12 cm.) below the top end and working up to where the star will be for 1-1/2 inches. Lay the balls slightly over one another to cover where you've pressed them into the wand.

Roll out 3 coils measuring 1/4 x 1 inches 2/3 x 2-1/2 cm.) and flatten them into leaf shapes, and press them onto the wand above the balls. Roll a 1-inch diameter bead and push it over the dowel and down to the

118

leaves. (It will flatten somewhat to more of a tube shape.) Bake according to the manufacturer's instructions

Begin decorating the other end of the dowel 4 inches (10 cm.) up from the bottom end, taking care not to break what you've already made. Roll a 1-1/4-inch (3-cm.) ball of clay and carefully work it onto the dowel. Form a 1/4- x 2-1/2-inch coil and connect the ends to form a tube shape and slide it onto the dowel next to the bead. Roll a 1-inch ball of clay and flatten it with the rolling pin to 2 inches. Slide it over the dowel and up the tube. Pinch the edges to ruffle and push firmly against the tube. Make small clay balls and attach them to the dowel in the same method as used at the top of the dowel. The balls should start 1-inch from the bottom and cover 1-1/4 inches up to the ruffle. Make

a few leaves to cover the top of the ball (grape) group.

Roll out an oval bead to 1-1/4 x 1-1/2 inches and push it onto the dowel lengthwise. Once it is firmly against the grapes, begin to twist it, starting at the top and working down, using your thumb and first 2 fingers. Twist it all the way to the tip, being careful not to twist it away from the grape cluster.

Repeat this procedure with another oval but twist it first and then attach the wide end at a right angle to the other twisted oval. Bake.

Paint the wand with the acrylic paint. Following the colors in the photo or choosing your own, paint the embossed stars and the tubed shape bead with just the gold paint pen. Paint next with the blue and so on. Spray with the acrylic high-shine sealer and then add highlights with the gold paint pen.

### Instructions for the Red and Gold Wand

Roll out a long 1/4-inch coil of clay and wrap it around the rod, attaching new coils to the old as you work. Wrap the entire rod and continue past the end. Coil the clay out from the end of the rod to form 1 spoke of the star. When you've wrapped a 2-inch

spoke, pull the clay end to form the star point

Form the other 3 spokes independently by coiling a 1-inch base and then continue for 2 more inches. Press these spokes into the center of the star. (See photo.) Make a small coil measuring 1 x 1/4 inches and attach 2 inches down from the top of the coil to indicate the end

*(continued on page 138)*

119

To create a pleasant transition from the living room, we continued the star theme into the dining room. The Rifkin's very contemporary approach to window treatments blends surprisingly well with their antiques, and we added holiday sparkle with bright felt banners decorated with stars. As a part of their everyday decor, the Rifkins had positioned full-sized, hand-carved menagerie animals from an 1800's carousel to soften the sides of the room, so we decorated the server and the window above the server to draw the carousel animals into the circle and make them become part of the celebration.

Because the toys in this room are so unique, we did our best to echo this uniqueness with some very special crafts. The Santa star ship was made by carving assorted shapes of foam and assembling them to create a ship. A magical full-size stuffed elf rides a carousel animal and an incredibly detailed angel was made from modeling compound.

## Stained Glass Stars

These simple tissue paper decorations introduce visitors to the home's star motif when they first come in the door.

### Materials

Black construction paper, craft glue, art tissue paper, plastic bag or other thin sheet of plastic, scissors

### Instructions

Trace the star pattern

Decide how many colors you'd like in your star. For a single color, simply cut out a piece of tissue that will cover the interior space of the star; for multi-colored stars, cut out 10 1-inch (2-1/2 cm.) pieces of tissue in assorted colors for each star.

from page 139 onto the construction paper and cut out the inner and outer edges. Dilute the craft glue with an equal amount of water in a small container. Cut the sides of the plastic bag open and tape the bag flat on a table.

Stir the glue mixture and pour a small amount onto the plastic. Spread the glue into an even film and press the black star into the glue to cover its entire surface. Next, spread the glue evenly onto the interior area of the star and press on overlapping pieces of tissue until the entire space is covered. (The colors will bleed and

enhance the finished appearance of your star.) Spread a thin layer of glue over the entire star and allow to dry overnight. Carefully remove the star from the plastic sheet and trim off any excess tissue. Hang in a window with tape or suction cups.

## Santa Star Ship

Since this year's Christmas gifts just might arrive on a star ship, you'll want to make sure your roof's landing pad is in A-1 condition. Although the instructions for this project look intimidating, the project is really fairly simple. Feel free to custom-design your own star ship with different shapes of foam, old watch parts, and small gears.

### Materials

8-inch (20-cm) foam ball and foam cone, 1- x 9- x 6-inch (2-1/2- x 22- x 15-cm.) sheet of foam for wings, back hatch, and instrument panel, glue gun, fine sandpaper, package of assorted model car gears, 10-inch (25-cm.) wooden propeller, 2 pieces of 3/16-inch metal tube (1 cut to 28 inches, 80 cm., and 1 cut to 14 inches (36 cm.), 4 2- x 3/16-inch wooden dowels, 28 inch x 12 inch sheet of aluminum flashing, 7/8-inch (2.2 cm.) blue metal tacks, red, green, and black acrylic paint, silver metallic paint, metal stars with clamps, 6 gold metallic pipe cleaners, wooden mini-size candle holder, 3- x 3-inch (7-1/2 cm.) piece of tag board or heavy paper, 12 inches (30 cm.) of gold, red, and green cording, 12- x 1/2-inch silver and black woven trim or ribbon, small clay beads, 1-1/2-inch metal wheel for steering wheel, heavy-gauge wire, small pieces of felt and fake fur, fabric or wooden Santa figure

### Instructions

Use a serrated knife to carve out a notch slightly less than 1/4 of the foam ball. (See pattern on page 139.) Cut the top 2 inches (5 cm.) off of the foam cone and put aside. Carve out a concave shape in the bottom of the large cone to make it fit snugly against the foam ball.

Carve out notches for Santa's legs (if necessary) according to the pattern. Hot-glue the cone to the ball, taking care to align the seat space on the ball, the foot space on the cone, and both of their imaginary lines.

Drive the metal tube through the center of the cone and the ball until it protrudes out both ends. You have now formed the body and nose of the ship. Carve out another concave shape in the remaining 2-inch cone section so that it fits snugly against the ball, and then slide it onto the metal tube to form the beginning of the ship's rear structure. Hot-glue into position.

Following the pattern on page 139, cut 2 rectangular pieces from the 1-inch foam to form the instrument and hatch panels. Cut and sand the wings according to the pattern. Insert the 14-inch (36 cm.) length of metal tube through the wings and body of the ship as shown in the diagram. Remove the metal tube and set aside.

Cut the aluminum flashing from the pattern and use the pieces to cover the instrument panel and rear hatch, gluing the metal on first and then reinforcing by pushing in the nails. Trace the instrument panel design onto the tag board, cut it out, and hot-glue it to the instrument panel foam. Braid all 3 colors of the cording together and hot-glue along the instrument panel to cover the tag board edge.

Insert 2 of the dowels 1 inch into the bottom foam of the instrument panel. Remove the dowels, add hot glue to the end, and reinsert, pushing the other end of the dowels into the nose cone. Remove, add hot glue, and reinsert, adding extra glue to the joint between the foam pieces.

Finish the hatch cover's edge with the silver braid trim and then attach it to the body of the ship following the same dowel and glue *(continued on page 139)*

# Elves

The real fun in making these whimsical, full-size elves comes from watching their unique personalities develop.

## Materials
Pair of children's size 6/8 red tights, pair of taupe or brown ladies' stockings, green t-shirt in children's size 8/10, 2 buttons (for eyes), 1/2 yard (.5 m) red flannel, green yarn, polyester stuffing, coat hanger, pink felt, cardboard

## Instructions
Using the patterns on page 149, cut out the hat, collar, belt, and lips from the red flannel, the eyes, gloves, and hat trim from the white flannel, and the nose and ears from the pink felt.

Trace the body form onto cardboard and cut it out. Stretch out the hanger and bend it to match the outline on the pattern. Place the cardboard legs into the

tights and fill out the shape with stuffing. Stuff the calf portions of the panty hose to form arms and stuff the hip portion of 1 side of the hose to form the head. Fit the stuffed hose onto the top of the cardboard form and tie up the excess with twist ties. The bulk of the hose will be covered by the clothing.

Fit the head and arms into the shirt. Pull the shirt down over the cardboard torso and fill out the chest area with stuffing. Tie a belt loosely around the midriff. Stitch the glove sections right sides together, turn right side out, and put the gloves over the hands. Place the collar around the neck and tack in place in the back. Sew the buttons in the center of the eyes. Position the nose and mouth and tack in place. Sew the hat seam. Fold the white hat trim in half lengthwise and stitch to the edge of the hat with right sides together. Turn right sides out, press, and tack the hat onto the head.

Tuck a piece of stuffing under the hat edges for hair. Make 3 pompons from the green yarn and tack them to the toes and the end of the hat. Finally, bend the elf's arms and head to a natural-looking position.

## Star Potholders

These simple potholders provide a burst of holiday color in the kitchen, and several of the steps are simple enough for kids to help.

### Materials

1 yard (.9 m) total of assorted holiday fabrics, quilt batting

### Instructions

Cut out an 8-inch (20-cm.) square for a backing fabric and 2 squares of quilt batting. Cut the remaining fabrics into rectangles measuring 8 x 6 inches (20 x 15 cm.). Fold each of the rect-angles as indicated in the illustration on page 150 and press. Fold the folded ends of the rectangles to a triangle point as indicated in the illustration and press again.

Place the batting layers on top of the fabric and carefully begin arranging the triangles on top of the batting, working from the center outward. (See piecing diagram on page 150.) Tack each of the points in place with thread before adding a new layer of points. When the base fabric is covered, turn it right side down and trim off any excess fabric. Finish with narrow strips of fabric cut on the bias.

## Window Banners

Simple felt banners can be decorated with graphic shapes, and make a lovely way to spice up windows or frame an archway.

### Materials

Felt, chalk, puff craft stars, sequin stars, metal clamp stars, gold or silver lame fabric, glue gun

### Instructions

Using a straight edge and a piece of chalk, mark off strips of felt 4-1/2 inches (11 cm.) wide and cut them to the length you need. Trim the felt strips to points on one end and fold the other end over 2 inches (5 cm.) and hot-glue down to form a casing.

Cut out the lame stars from the pattern on page 139. Play with the arrangement of the lame stars, puff stars, sequin stars, and metal stars until you like the design. Attach the metal stars with their clamps and the other stars with hot glue. Insert your curtain rod or a tension rod through the casing in the felt strips.

## Silver Birch Topiary

This contemporary topiary works great on a table with overhead lighting because it creates fascinating shadows.

### Materials

30- x 1-inch (75- x 2-1/2-cm.) straight birch branch for the trunk, approximately 30 birch twigs, 3-inch (7-1/2-cm.) foam ball, glue gun, Spanish moss, plaster of Paris, plastic pot, thin-gauge spool wire, small pressure sensitive metallic stars, silver metallic thread, silver spray paint, silver glitter spray, opalescent tinsel

### Instructions

Mix the plaster of Paris and pour into the plastic container. Center the branch and hold it in place until the plaster firms. Cut a hole in the bottom of the foam ball deep enough to insert the birch branch in 1 inch (2-1/2 cm.). Fill part of the hole with hot glue and insert the birch branch. Cover the base and the pot with moss and secure the moss in place by wrapping with wire.

Cover the foam ball with moss and hold the moss in place by wrapping around the ball several times with wire. Begin inserting the twigs into the ball, starting at the bottom and moving up toward the top center, hot-gluing them in position and placing them very close to each other.

When the ball is completely covered with twigs, spray it with silver spray paint. Spray the base with silver paint. Attach the stars back to back over the metallic string. Cut the star-covered string to varying lengths and hot-glue them onto the lower branches. Spray the entire tree, including the trunk, with silver glitter and finish with a little opalescent tinsel.

## Star Candle Holders

These brilliant silver candle holders create an instant party atmosphere when the candles are lit by casting star shadows on the table. For a dressier look, add some opalescent tinsel to the candle holders.

### Materials

1/4 x 10 inch (2/3 x 25 cm.) piece of plywood, 1-1/2- x 5-inch (4- x 12-cm.) piece of plywood, white latex base paint, silver spray paint, medium-gauge silver spool wire, glue gun

### Instructions

Using the patterns on page 139, cut 5 small stars from 1/4-inch plywood. Cut the large star from 1-1/2-inch plywood. Drill 1/16-inch holes in the bottom of each of the small stars and the tips of the large star. Then drill a 3/4-inch (2-cm.) hole for the candle in the center of the larger star as indicated on the patterns. Sand all edges.

Paint the stars with a base coat and then spray paint with silver. Assemble the stars using with the wire and secure with hot glue. Last, form graceful curves in the wire.

## Winter Wreath

The floral arrangement in this wreath forms a subtle star, making it blend in beautifully with the other star projects in the room without being too obvious.

### Materials

16-inch (41-cm.) foam wreath base, fresh-cut boxwood, floral picks, dried German statice, dried cockscomb, dried hydrangea, dried love-in-a-mist, 5 white silk roses, glue gun, floral tape

### Instructions

Gather the boxwood into small bunches of 3 stems each and attach each bunch to a floral pick. Cover the wire on the floral picks with floral tape. Insert the picks snugly into the base at an angle, positioning each new pick to cover the stem of the previous pick.

Arrange the cockscomb heads on top of the boxwood to form an even star pattern and then hot-glue them in place. Hot-glue the hydrangea in between the cockscomb and then hot-glue a silk rose in the center of each hydrangea section. Last, fill in any bare spots with the love-in-a-mist.

## Serving Table Floral Swag

This lush swag works well as a centerpiece on a serving table or as a garland over a doorway. When the holidays are over, just remove the stars for a year 'round decoration.

### Materials

36-inch (89-cm.) length of thick raffia braid that's been fastened on each end, floral picks, floral tape, 2 large bunches of dried German statice, 3 bunches of dried cockscomb, 1 bunch of dried hydrangea, 1 bunch of dried love-in-a-mist seed heads, 12 small craft puff stars

### Instructions

Cut the German statice into 6-inch (15-cm.) lengths and arrange into small bouquets of 3 to 5 stems each. Attach the bouquets to floral picks and tape over the picks' wire. Insert the picked bouquets of German statice into the edges of the braid, reinforcing with hot glue if necessary, starting from each end and working evenly toward the center.

Hot-glue individual stems of cockscomb down the center of the braid, and then hot-glue bits of hydrangea between the statice and cockscomb. Last, fill in any blank spaces with the love-in-a-mist and hot-glue in the stars.

## Children's Tree Decorating Apron

Because all children love the mystery and intrigue of pockets, this Christmas tree apron has a row of small pockets just perfect for holiday tidbits and surprises or to hold Christmas ornaments when decorating the tree.

### Materials

Purchased apron (or pattern, fabric, and the necessary sewing notions), small piece of matching or contrasting fabric for pockets, narrow green ribbon, narrow elastic, washable markers or fabric crayons

### Instructions

Cut out the tree segments and the pocket using the patterns on page 149. Applique the top segment of the tree in place with a contrasting thread, inserting a 2-inch (5-cm.) length of green ribbon under 1 corner before stitching to form the loop.

Hem the top edge of the 2nd tier, position another ribbon loop at the opposite corner, and applique the remaining 3 edges in place. Finish the last 2 tiers of the tree and the trunk with the technique described above.

Form the pocket folds as indicated on the pattern (box-pleat style) and press in place. Baste the pleats in place 3/8 of an inch (1 cm.) from the bottom edge. Zig-zag or serge the top edge of the pocket and press under half an inch (1-1/3 cm.) and sew to form a casing.

Baste the pocket on the apron, leaving the ends of the casing free. Insert the elastic into the casing, pull it through, and secure the ends. Adjust the elastic so the small end sections of the pocket are flat and stitch along the sewing lines for these 2 sections.

Adjust the elastic evenly across the remaining sections, pin in place, and stitch along the sewing lines. Finish the top edge with bias tape. Allow the child to decorate the apron with washable markers or fabric crayons.

# Santa Apron

This festive cooking apron was designed to do more than just look pretty.

The Santa patch was strategically positioned in the area where most cooking spills will occur and the coated surface of the Santa wipes clean with a wet towel.

### Materials

Purchased apron (or a pattern, fabric, and the necessary sewing notions), iron-on Santa t-shirt patch (or adhesive interfacing and a small piece of fabric with large holiday motifs)

### Instructions

Try the apron on and stand in front of a mirror to determine the best position for the iron-on. Attach the iron-on to the apron per the manufacturer's instructions.

## Mirror Candle Stand

This lovely candle stand looks perfect displayed in an entryway arrangement of family pictures and wreaths, and the mirror doubles the candle's light.

### Materials

1/2- x 10- x 15-inch (1-1/4- x 25 x 39 cm.) piece of wood, 1/2- x 5- x 5-inch (1-1/4- x 12- x 12-cm.) piece of wood, 1/2-inch cove molding, acrylic craft paint, 5- x 7-inch (12- x 17-cm.)mirror, 4 1-inch (2-1/2-cm.) screws, wood glue or glue gun, gold metallic paint, wood stain, sandpaper

### Instructions

Build the stand according to the plans on page 154. Paint the frame red and allow the paint to dry completely. Paint the molding and the edges around the mirror green. Then trace a star onto the top of the mirror and paint it gold and green.

After the paint is dry, rub gold paint on the molding and around the mirror itself with a rag. (This coat of gold shouldn't be too thick, but just enough to look like it's coming off.)

If an aged look is desired, sand the stand with garnet paper to rub off some of the paint. Brush on a coat of provincial stain and wipe off any excess with a dry, lint-free rag. Position the mirror in place and secure by gluing in small blocks to the sides.

## Eileen B. Stared

Inspired by Pre-Raphaelite portraits, this angel is the perfect decoration for a doorway because her long, lean lines don't infringe on head space. She may look difficult, but if you can roll clay into logs and balls, you'll have no trouble making it.

### Materials

Tissue paper, craft knife, 3 pounds of white low-fire modeling compound, several small packets of low-fire modeling compound in red, pink, purple, copper, green, blue, and yellow, 1/4-inch (2/3-cm.) foam core board measuring 1/4 x 12 x 60 inches (2/3 x 30 x 150 cm.), acrylic paints in black, ultramarine blue, burnt umber, and red, gold metallic paint, gold metallic pen, 6 mm imitation pearls, narrow ribbon, pressure sensitive stars, miniature jingle bell (for earring), 18- x 10-inch (46- x 25-cm.) sheet of uncorrugated cardboard covered smoothly with aluminum foil, rolling pin, 2 pieces of 1/4-inch and 3/8-inch wood stripping at least 20 inches (50 cm.) long, plastic clay tools (available in packets where modeling compound is sold), tube of adhesive cement that won't dissolve foam core

### Instructions

Trace the angel pattern on pages 154 through 159 onto tissue in 3 17-inch (43-cm.) sections. Each section is constructed and baked separately and then assembled later. The clay is rolled out over the foil-covered cardboard, and the wood strips are positioned on the edges of the cardboard so the ends of the rolling pin can rest on them, thus ensuring an even thickness of clay.

### Section I

(1) Roll out a piece of clay on the cardboard to 8 x 18 x 1/4 inches (20 x 46 x 2/3 cm.). Place the tissue patterns for the star, arm, and head sections on top of the clay and use a craft knife to cut their outlines through the tissue

Outline the thumb with a pencil pressed lightly through the tissue into the clay. Remove the tissue.

(2) Mix a 1-1/2 inch (4-cm.) ball of white clay with just a touch of copper and red clays until you have a flesh tone. Roll the ball into a very long shape. Cover the arms and hand area with this clay, smoothing the pieces together to form a smooth layer. (Mix more clay if necessary.)

Make the thumb by rolling out a 1-1/2-inch (4-cm.) log that is fatter at 1 end than the other. Press the log into position, consulting the tissue for the exact size and location, and flatten slightly. Draw the finger nail with a pointed plastic tool and smooth the other end into the hand.

**Star and Sleeve.** Leave the star shape white and add texture to it by smoothing on small bits of clay.

(3) Form 3 clay logs 1/4 x 3 inches long of red clay, purple clay, and green clay. Roll the red log flat to measure 1- x 4- x 1/16-inch (2-1/2- x 10- x 1/6-cm.). Press a piece of lace (or paper doily) into this patterned piece of clay with a rolling pin.

(4) Remove the lace and the press it into the sleeve in the same manner.

(5) Next attach the 1-inch strips of clay to the sleeve end, ruffling it as you go and looping the ends under. Use the plastic tool to press the sleeve end of lace into the sleeve a little to bond. Cover the area where the lace and sleeve connect with green and purple logs.

**Face.** Mix together a 1-1/2-inch white clay ball with a small amount of red and copper clay. Roll out the ball and coat the face with it. Spread in a dot of pink clay to highlight the cheek area. Using more pink clay and the face pattern, create the lips by rolling 2 tiny logs, pinching them together at one end and then pressing and flattening them into position. Form the eye by mixing the desired color into a 1/8-inch round ball and pressing it into position. Position the bell earring and press into the clay. Remove the bell and set aside.

**Halo/Hat.** Roll out a 2- x 3-inch (5- x 7-1/2 cm.) oval of clay to 1/16-inch thickness. Position and gather the lower edges. Using a plastic tool, press this clay together with the base along the lower edge of the hair and along the sides of the halo shape. Do not press the facing surface down as a puffy look is desirable.

**Hair.** Roll out a 1-1/2- x 2-inch oval of copper clay and smooth it into position to form the cap of the hair. Press in place and trim off the excess. Mix tiny amounts of copper with a few different colors and roll them out into miniature logs measuring 1/16 x 1-1/2 inches. Attach them to the sleeve at the forehead in a wave pattern. (Refer to photo.) Trim the ends if necessary and press the logs into place.

(6) Roll out copper logs measuring 1/8 x 2 inches and flatten them with a rolling pin. Position the strips in place from the hair cap to the shoulder, looping and curling every once in a while.

**Net Hat with Pearls.** Roll out 1/8-inch pink and yellow logs. Weave them over cap of the hair and press them in place. Roll out pink, yellow, and blue clay logs to 1/8- x 4-inch pieces. Twist them together and form a soft arch to frame the face. Press lightly in position and tuck in the ends. Press the pearls in where the coils cross. (Note: You may need to glue the pearls in later to keep them from falling out.) Make sure that the cut where the head section and the body join together is still crisp and then bake on the foil-covered cardboard according to manufacturer's directions.

When the baked clay has cooled, paint in the ear and eye detail with brown and black acrylic paint and glue on earring. The sleeve will be painted later. Using the gold paint pen, color the hat/halo and star and glue on any loose pearls.

*Note:* The remaining instructions use the same techniques as described in the steps above. The steps are referenced by the number in parentheses at the end of a sentence.

Repeat the general directions from step 1 using the tissues for the center sections. Coat the arm by repeating the first part of step 2. Press lace into the sleeve and tunic in the same manner explained in steps 3 and 4. Make the lace trim for the sleeve as explained in steps 3 and 5. Twist together 1/8-inch logs of pink, blue, and yellow clay to form the bodice decoration. Trim the ends and press lightly into the clay, consulting the photo for position.

**Collar.** The collar is made the same way as the sleeve lace (but without the gathering) Place cords of clay on the top and bottom as shown in the photo.

**Wings.** Mix several balls of clay in light pastel colors. (Create the pastel colors by adding small amounts of yellow, blue, and pink to the white clay.) Roll the balls into 1/4- x 1-inch cords. Press the clay with your fingertips to form feather shapes, pinching slightly at the tops. With a pointed plastic tool, draw on a few feather-like lines. Press the feathers into the wing section starting at the bottom

and working your way up the top and in toward the body. Press the base of the feathers into the clay, overlapping as you go and varying the colors at random.

**Lace Trim for Tunic Bottom.** This piece is made the same way as the cuff lace in steps 3 & 5. Use pink clay for the lace and yellow clay for the cording. Pearls have been added between the cording and lace. A twist of yellow, pink, and blue cording was also added to the bottom edge of the lace.

**Hair.** Follow the directions in step 6, but let the ribbons twine for a longer distance. Use a plastic tool to press the underside of the loops to the white clay. This section is now ready to bake.

### Section III

Repeat the general directions from step 1 with the lower dress and slipper tissue. Using a pencil, mark the bottom of the dress on the leg and the inside of the slipper. Using the mixing technique from step 2 and cover the leg with flesh tone.

Roll out a 1-inch ball of pink clay and use it to cover the slipper.

Then place a 2-inch ribbon of clay at the heal of the slipper. Press in a yellow clay cord approximately 12 inches long x 1/8 inches wide around the top edge of the slipper. Now use a pointed tool to imitate stitching lines along this cord and on both sides of the ribbon of clay on the slipper's heel.

Roll 2 1/8- x6-inch cords of yellow clay flat to make the slipper ties. Position the criss-crosses of yellow ribbon and press in place. Add the

**Tip**
Arrange fresh-cut boxwood (or other greenery) and red silk roses on top of a cabinet to add a subtle, but definite holiday touch in a dark, high corner.

bow loops only. The ruffle at the bottom of the dress is made in the same manner as the sleeve lace in steps 3 and 5. Section III is now ready to bake.

**Assembly and Finishing**
Working on a flat, protected surface, position all 3 baked sections on the foam core. Check to make sure they fit snugly together. If not, trim down the clay with a craft knife until a better fit is accomplished.

Cement the 3 sections to the foam core, carefully pressing them snugly to the foam core and making sure

they fit together well. Cut away the excess foam core around the angel and her star with a craft knife.

Paint the dress in two separate steps. First, thin the ultramarine paint with water until it's the consistency of water and use it to paint the sleeve, tunic, and lower portion of the dress. Dab some of the surface of the sleeve and tunic with a paper towel, leaving the lace highlights white. While the paint is still very wet and puddly on the lower part of the dress, drop on some metallic gold, non-water based paint. When the paint on

the tunic and sleeve has dried, go over it with a very watery coat of black acrylic paint to further show off the lace patterns.

Highlight areas like the wings, lace, ruffles, and hair with the gold paint pen. Glue on the ribbon and stars to the back of the foot bow as shown in the photo. Last, cut the wood strip in half and glue it to the back of the foam core, overlapping the strips above each other where they meet for 4-1/2 inches. Drill holes down through the wood strip and attach a hanger. Paint the entire back black.

137

of the 5th spoke. (Paint it green later to match the other star tips.) Roll a 1-inch ball and press a 3/4-inch (2-cm.) plastic gem into its center until the gem is surrounded by clay. Place this in the center of the star and press on the gem until a bond is formed between the clay pieces. Roll a 1/2-inch ball and attach it to the bottom end of the wand. Make some 1/2-inch leaves and attach them between the ball and the cord. Bake.

When cool, paint the wand gold, red, and green. (See photo for precise color locations.) When the paint has dried, wrap the wand's stem with red satin cord, starting at the top back and gluing as needed. Leave 4 inches of trailing cord to glue the stars onto.

### Instructions for the White, Green, and Red Wand

This wand is by far the fastest and easiest to make. First roll out a long strip of white clay from a 1- x 14-inch (2-1/2- x 36-cm.) coil. Don't worry about the shape but try to keep the thickness to 1/8 of an inch. Wrap the clay strip up the 1/4-inch dowel, adding length as needed. As you get to the top, just let the ends flop to form the star points. Add additional pieces of clay folded over to form the other points and pressed into the back. Fold the clay softly for a natural, easy look. (See photo.)

Roll the tip of the points in toward the center and lift the star's points to give a slight wave to the clay. Attach 1/8- x various lengths of clay coils 1/8-inch in diameter here and there as though they were coming out of the clay folds. Make rings of clay with coils and slide

them onto the very end of the dowel, adding a little squiggle of clay to form the very end. Make a small star and attach it to the stem of the wand about 4-1/2 inches from the bottom tip. Bake

When cool, paint the wand, referring the photo for color. Leave the white areas unpainted. The edges are highlighted with a gold paint pen and so is the tiny star. Spray on a coat of clear acrylic high-shine spray. Tie on the satin cord and add jingle bells to the ends.

### Instructions for the Purple, Red, and Gold Star Wand

This wand is made using techniques similar to the blue, red, and gold wand. The main difference is the star itself, which is made from a 2-inch ball of clay (star center) and 5 1- x 3-inch logs of clay that have been stood on end and tamped on a work surface to form a fat end and then rolled at the other end until a skinny, wormy point is created. The fat ends of these logs are then pushed into the 2-inch ball, flattening the ball on the facing side and creating a pentagon shape when the sides are pushed in. (See photo).

Roll out 3 coils of clay to measure 1/8 x 10 inches and flatten them with a rolling pin to form 1/8-inch ribbon. Press the ribbons into the star over the pentagon's center, referring to the photo for position. The decorations on the wand are made in the same way as the grape balls in the first wand but the ball is pressed with your finger tips more in the center to form a concave shape. (See photo.)

Finish with clay beads in round, tubular, or teardrop shapes. Create a different shape by rolling out a 1/4- x 3-inch circle from a 1-1/2-inch ball and cutting out a star.

Pierce the tips of this star about 1/4 of an inch in from the edge using a pencil to make the holes large enough to thread satin cord through. Force this star piece through its center and onto the dowel. Add a few more beads and then push on the star itself. Note: You may have to support all of this between 2 clay stands that work like sawhorses to hold the dowel rod and make it easier to work on those 3-dimensional shapes. You can bake these "horses" so that they will be sturdier.

Bake.

Paint with acrylic paints and highlight with metallic gold paint

and then coat with a layer of clear, high-shine acrylic spray. Insert the satin cord into the holes and glue. Glue mini bells to the cord ends.

### Materials for Court Jester

3/16-x 4- x 18-inch piece of balsa wood, 2 mini bells, plastic gem star, 1/16- x 4-inch straight wire, acrylic paint, brushes, black paint pen, craft knife, tissue, pencil, white glue, red satin cord, 1-inch clay bead

### Instructions

Trace the pattern pieces from page 154. Re-trace the pattern onto the balsa wood and cut it out with a craft knife. Follow the pattern and photo to paint the figure and the bead. When the paint is dry, sharpen the edges of your paint with a black paint pen. Paint, wire, and glue on the star. Assemble and glue the figure following the pattern. Glue the satin cord with the bead attached to the back of the jester.

### Materials for Star Wand Display Board

1- x 24- x 34-inch (2-1/2- x 60- x 86-cm.) plywood board with a smoothly finished face, 1- and 2-

inch flat paint brushes, craft paints in red, green, and brilliant orange, walnut stain, 14 plastic craft gem stars, 4 sets of curtain rod holders, sandpaper, black spray paint

## Instructions

Cut an arch 2 feet (60 cm.) in diameter at 1 end of the plywood. Sand and paint the board green. Mark off a 1-inch boarder all the way around the board edge using a straight edge and a pencil. Do the arch using the tip instructions on page 89. Paint the border red. When the paint is dry, wipe on the stain. When the stain has dried, measure off 1-inch squares every 1-9/16 inches and paint them brilliant orange. Then glue the plastic gem stars in the middle of each.

Spray the curtain rod holders black and attach them to the board, spacing them to fit your wands. Glue on the jester and hang the board with a wire hanger.

### SANTA STAR SHIP

*(continued from page 123)*

procedure described above. Cut additional squares and triangles of flashing similar to those shown as examples in the pattern and use them to cover the entire nose cone and ball, gluing on and overlapping each piece as you go. Do the cone ends first, clipping pieces of flashing to go from the cone end up over the ball. (See sample flashing pieces.) Mark the holes through the flashing where the wings attach. Press in or hammer the tacks as shown in the photo and reinforce with dabs of hot glue if needed.

*(continued on page 140)*

Instrument and hatch (Enlarge 200%)

## Southwest Star Ornaments
Page 116

### Instructions

Enlarge the pattern to measure 5-1/2 inches (13 cm.) top to bottom. Place the pattern over the tag board and mark the 11 dots on the star with a push pin, being careful not to move the pattern. Score lightly along the dashed lines with a craft knife on the front and back of the star. Cut out along the solid lines. Fold gently along the scored line and glue the tabs of the 2 stars together.

## Candle Holder
Page 127

### Instructions

Enlarge the dashed line star pattern to measure 5-1/2 inches (13 cm.) top to bottom for the base; then enlarge the pattern to measure 2-3/4 inches (7 cm.) for the small stars.

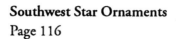

Back

Front

Holes (11 in all)

Tabs

## Stained Glass Stars
Page 122

### Instructions

Enlarge the dashed lines to measure 8 inches (20 cm.) top to bottom.

100%

100%

100%

Side View

Wing

Wing · cut 2

Instrument panel (enlarge 200%)

Front View

*(continued from page 139)*

Glue a piece of felt into Santa's seat and trim with fake fur. Paint the gears with the acrylic paints and slide them, the clay beads, and the propeller onto the metal tube and secure with hot glue if needed. (You may have to drill larger holes into the gears so they'll fit over the tube.)

Cover the wings with aluminum flashing and create a trim on the top of the wings by bending scallop-shaped pieces of metal upward and then gluing them to the wing starting at the back and progressing forward, overlapping as you go. Slide the metal tube through the body of the ship and then slide the wings into position. Secure with hot glue. Attach the gears to the tip of the tube and secure with hot glue.

Paint the candle holder silver and attach it to the nose of the ship. Secure with a gear and hot glue. Add additional trims such as the steering wheel, stars, and miscellaneous communication or directional equipment. Fill any gaps in the fuselage with hot glue and paint the hardened glue with silver paint. Now you're ready to fly! Attach double lengths of metallic pipe cleaners or mono filament to 3 points on the ship for hanging and blast off!

## Fireplace Screen
Page 12

### Materials for Screen Front
4 half rounds measuring 1/2 x 23-1/2 inches (1-1/4 x 59 cm.)

4 half rounds measuring 1/2 x 10-1/2 inches (1-1/4 x 26 cm.)

2 half rounds measuring 1/2 x 11-1/2 inches (1-1/4 x 28 cm.)

2 quarter rounds measuring 1/4 x 10-1/2 inches (6 mm x 26 cm.)

1 quarter rounds measuring 1/4 x 11-1/2 inches (6 mm x 28 cm.)

2 arches 11 inches (27 cm.) in diameter cut from 1/2-inch plywood (interior diameter should be 10 inches, 25 cm.)

1 arch 12 inches (30 cm.) in diameter cut from 1/2-inch plywood (interior diameter should be 11 inches)

4 2-inch (5-cm.) wood craft wheels

2 1/4-inch (6-mm) wood craft wheels

1 piece of wood measuring 2 x 4 x 38 inches (5 x 10 x 98 cm.)

glue gun

Instruction for tins on page 12

140

## Materials for Back

4 pieces of wood measuring 1 x 2 x 23-1/2 inches (2-1/2 x 5 x 59 cm.)

4 pieces of wood measuring 1 x 2 x 10-1/4 inches (2-1/2 x 5 x 25 cm.)

2 pieces of wood measuring 1 x 2 x 11-1/4 inches (2-1/2 x 5 x 27 cm.)

1 piece of wood measuring 1 x 1 x 11-1/4 inches

2 pieces of wood measuring 1 x 1 x 10-1/4 inches

2 arches 11 inches (27 cm.) in diameter cut from 1/2-inch (1-1/4 cm.) plywood (interior diameter should be 10 inches, 25 cm.)

1 arch 12 inches (30 cm.) in diameter cut from 1/2-inch plywood (interior diameter should be 11 inches)

6 triangles measuring 3 x 3 x 3 x 1 inches (7-1/2 x 7-1/2 x 7-1/2 x 2-1/2 cm.)

8 2-1/2-inch (6-cm.) Philip's head dry wall nails

Box of #6 finishing nails

Box of 1/2-inch tacks

## Instructions

Cut all wood to size. Spray paint the 1 x 2s, 1 x 1s, back arches, and wood triangles black. Route or round the front and sides of the 2 x 4 x 38. If you choose to round the edges, use a plane to ease them and then sand smooth. Screw the base to the vertical members using dry wall screws. Attach the cross members with finishing nails. Square up the structure and glue in triangular supports. Tack the tins into position. Glue the half and quarter rounds, the craft wheels, and the arches over the tacks and into position. Glue the back arches to the tins and the top edges of the 1 x 2s. Tack the arches to the 1 x 2s as well. Paint and finish according to the directions on page 12.

1/2" x 1/2" x 12" d
1/2" x 1/2" x 11" d
10 1/2" x 1/2" half round
1/2" x 23 1/2" half round
11 1/2" x 1/2" half round
10 1/2" x 1/2" half round
10 1/2" x 1/4" quarter round
2" x 4" x 38"

1/2" x 1/2" x 12" d
1/2" x 1/2" x 11" d
10 1/4" x 1" x 2"
1" x 2" x 23 1/2"
11 1/4" x 1" x 2"
10 1/4" x 1" x 2"
10 1/4" x 1" x 1"
3" x 3" x 3" x 1"
2" x 4" x 38"
glue in

Screen Back

**Magic Sleigh**
Page 13

**Materials**

1 piece of wood measuring 1 x 6 x 29 inches (2-1/2 x 15 x 52 cm.)

2 pieces of wood measuring 1 x 6 x 31 inches (2-1/2 x 15 x 77 cm.)

2 pieces of wood measuring 1 x 12 x 52 inches (2-1/2 x 30 x 132 cm.)

3 pieces of wood measuring 1 x 4 x 15 inches (2-1/2 x 10 x 39 cm.)

30 2-inch (5-cm.) flat head screws

Enlarge 400%

51 inches (121 cm.)

## Country Sleigh
Page 89

### Instructions

Cut all wood to size and sand. Screw the sleigh's top boards to the cross members and then the runners to the cross support ends. Paint and finish according to the directions on page 13.

Enlarge 400%

Enlarge 260%

**Firewood Storage Box**
Page 43

Top Line Center

← curve of side

12 inches

38 inches

12

Lid

**Kilim Place Mat**
Page 49

yellow....
red......
blue.....
green....

144

## Santa's Serving Tray
Page 95

### Instructions

Enlarge the patterns on a copy machine 400%. Transfer the patterns to the wood, tracing the arms separately. Cut out Santa's helper, arms, tray, and base. Sand all pieces. Follow the painting directions on page 95 and then screw the arms, base, and tray together.

## Christmas Bird's Home
Page 100

Enlarge the pattern on a copy machine 200%. Transfer the pattern to the wood and cut out all pieces. Cut a hole in the front piece using a drill and jig or saber saw. Drill a hole for the perch with a 3/8-inch (1 cm.) drill. Nail the front to the sides, turn over, and nail the back to the sides. Nail on the bottom. Set all nails and fill with putty. Nail the roof pieces together and then nail the roof to the house. Nail the chimney pieces together, position, and glue them to the roof. Paint according to the directions on page 100.

Enlarge 400%

2½"

2¼"

4"

Enlarge 400%

Side pieces 3-½ x 4-½ inches
(8-¼ x 11¼ cm)
Roof 7 x 7 inches
and 7 x 6-¼ inches
(17 x 15.65 cm)
Bottom 4-3/8 x 5-3/4
inches (10 x 14 cm)

Enlarge 200%

Enlarge 400%

Enlarge 150%

**Papier-Mâché Angel**
Page 88

Gold Boardered Multi-Color
B  Ultramarine Blue
LB Light Blue
PP Pale Peach
Y  Pale Yellow
P  Pink
G  Green
L  Lavender
R  Red
F  Flesh
DF Deep Flesh
Br Brown
O  Orange
W  White
X  Gold

**Victorian Santa Frame**
Page 32

Enlarge 200%

Enlarge to 48-inches (116.5 cm)

Metalic Pipe Cleaners

Metalic Pipe Cleaners

Metalic Pipe Cleaners

size to one half of your window width

**Braid and Tassel Window Treatment**

Page 40

*Enlarge 200%.*

Inner Fold  Inner Fold  Top stich  28-inches (68 cm.) of elastic  Enlarge patter 300%
Outer Fold  Outer Fold  Top Stich  or to fit

enter fold

Pocket Face          Pocket Face

Inner Fold        Inner Fold        Outer Fold

Pocket Pattern for Apron
Page 130

Clothespin Furniture
Page 106

Elves
Page 14

Enlarge
Figure
Hat, Hatband
and collar
800%

fold

Chair - Side View          Chair  Front View

collar

Hat

100%

Hat trim & belt

Mouth          100%

Mouth          100%          Ear

100%          Eyes          glove

Mouth          100%

149

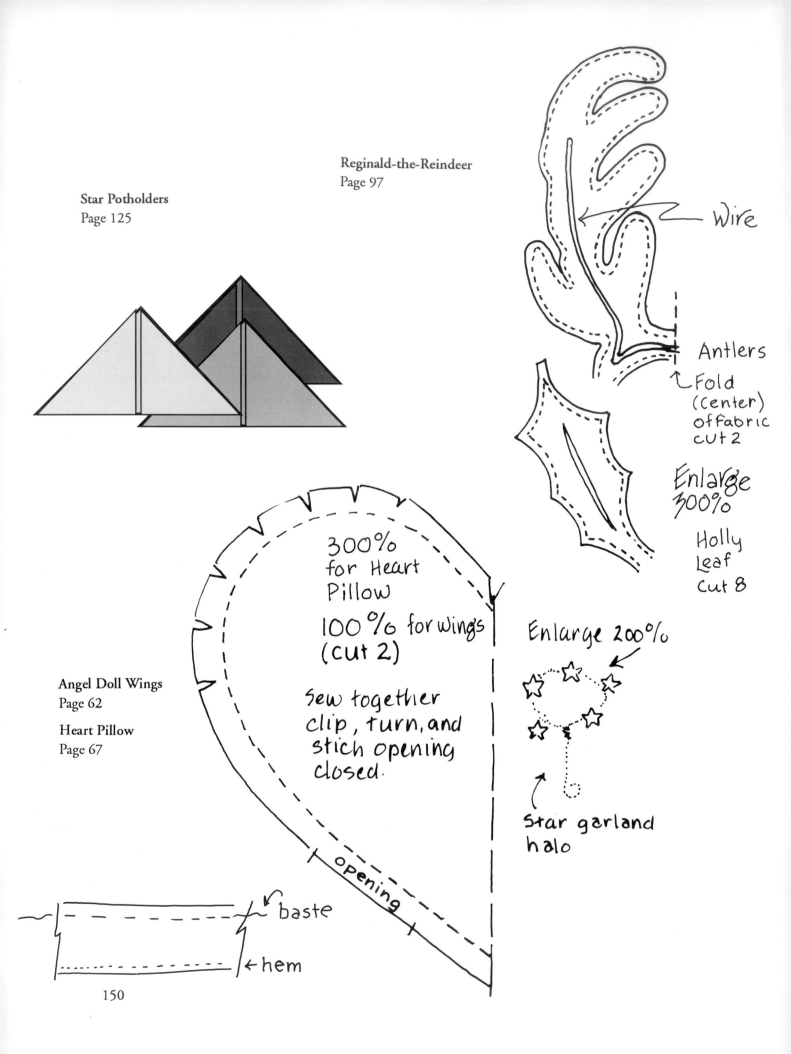

Star Potholders
Page 125

Reginald-the-Reindeer
Page 97

Wire

Antlers
Fold
(center)
of fabric
cut 2

Enlarge
300%

Holly
Leaf
Cut 8

300%
for Heart
Pillow
100% for wings
(cut 2)

Sew together
clip, turn, and
stich opening
closed.

Enlarge 200%

Star garland
halo

Angel Doll Wings
Page 62

Heart Pillow
Page 67

opening

baste

hem

**Starland Garland**
Page 98

Star Front and Back
Enlarge 200%

Wreath Front
and Back
Enlarge 200%

**Santa Chicken**
Page 93

Ribbon
loop

Fold

Red felt
sewn into
seam at
top
cut 2

Enlarge 200%

Fold

Cut 2

Cut 4

Fold back flap
& stitch to
body

Bell

cut 2

Legs cut 2

Opening

Fold line

## Quilt
Page 100

Fleece Pattern
cut 2

Ears
cut 2

tail

**Sweatshirt Tree**
Page 103

Enlarge 200%

Trunk

Red
Felt

Trim

**Teddy Bear Garland**
Pages 107, 108

Ornaments
Page 107

sheep Body
Pattern

Laundry Bag, Tree Skirt,
and Pillow Case
Pages 104, 105

100%
For
Pillow case
300%
For
Laundry
Bag
125%
For Tree
Skirt

100%

Laundry bag
Stocking

Cut 6
For 2½-
inch
(6.35 cm.)
Ball

Ornaments
Place Mats
Page 36

Reference Star

Center Line    Enlarge 400%

153

**Eileen B. Starred**
Page 133

100%

**The Jester**
Page 119

Enlarge 200%

**Christmas Mirror**
Page 133

**Terra Cotta Pot Bells**
Page 117

Enlarge 250%

**Instructions**
Enlarge the pattern 250% on a copy machine and transfer onto the wood pieces. Cut out using a band or jig saw. (To cut out area for mirror, drill holes in corners first, then cut.) Sand and nail all pieces in place. Paint according to the instructions on page 133. Position the mirror, holding in place with 1 x 1-1/2 pieces of wood glued to the frame behind the mirror. Turn the mirror over and cut. Holding it in position, attach the molding around the mirror. (Using a little extra molding, cut your 45 degree angle miter as a test so that you get it right in the finished piece.)

Enlarge 200%

Candle Stand Top

Candle Stand Base

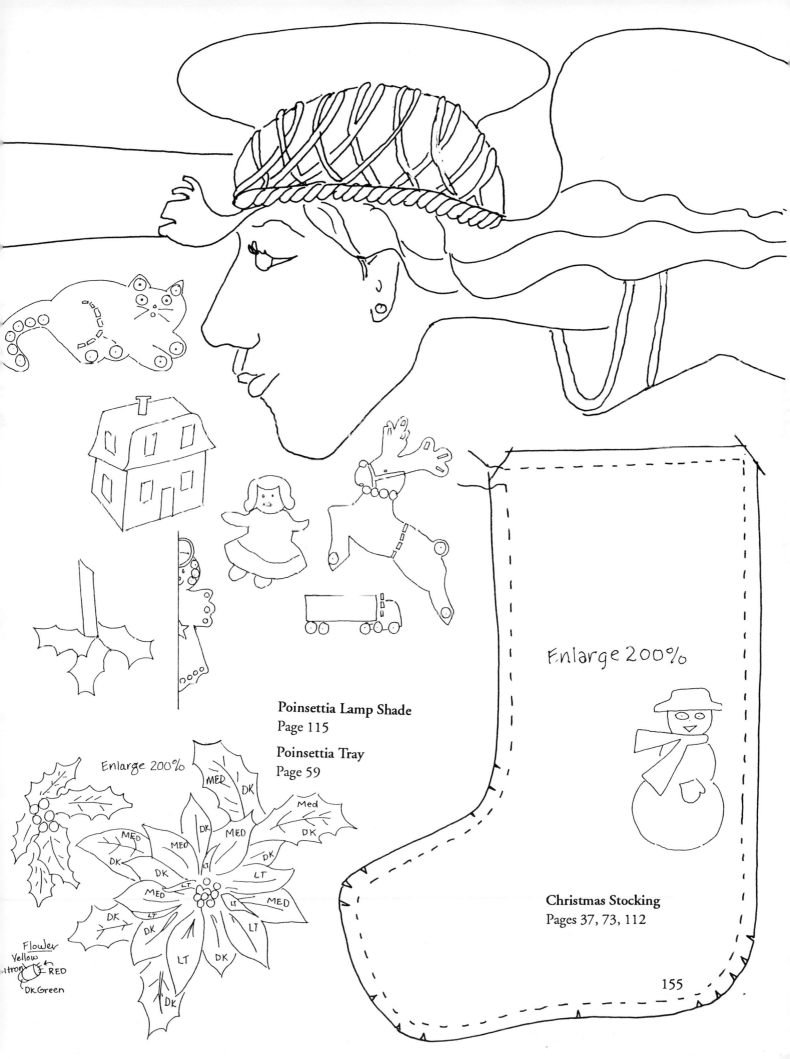

**Poinsettia Lamp Shade**
Page 115

**Poinsettia Tray**
Page 59

Enlarge 200%

Enlarge 200%

MED  DK

Med

DK

MED

DK

MED

DK

DK

MED

MED

DK

LT

LT

DK

LT

MED

DK

LT

LT

LT

DK

LT

DK

LT

DK

DK

Flower
Yellow
Citron  RED
Dk.Green

**Christmas Stocking**
Pages 37, 73, 112

155

## Materials and Techniques

Following is a discussion of many of the materials and techniques used to complete the projects in A Fireside Christmas. Experienced crafters may wish to skim through this section for expert tips and information on many of the new craft products on the market. Inexperienced crafters may wish to read through the instructions and experiment with the materials a few times before beginning an actual project.

### Working with Dried Materials...

If you come across a project materials' list that calls for dried roses, globe amaranth, or some other dried flower, (and you didn't happen to dry these materials from you summer garden last year), you'll be happy to discover that many craft stores sell a wide variety of dried flowers, herbs, and preserved greenery. You can always substitute one pretty bloom for another in any project.

### Floral Picks, Pins, and Tape

As their name implies, these handy craft tools were developed by florists because they save time and make the finished product look more professional. They're not expensive and you can find them in most craft stores in several shades of brown and green.

### Floral Wire

This versatile wire can be found in pre-cut lengths or on spools.

For stems of dried flowers or herbs that are too short or too weak, you can create a stronger, longer stem made from wire by holding a piece of floral wire against the top of the stem and securing the two together by spiraling a piece of floral tape down over the stem and the wire. Pulling gently on the tape as you work will stretch it and cause it to adhere.

Many wreath and arrangement projects call for floral picks. The tapered end on a wooden floral pick inserts easily into foam, moss, and straw bases. The thin-gauge wire that comes attached to the floral pick allows you to secure just one or as many as three to five stems to the pick. To secure a small bouquet of flowers (or a single stem) to a pick, position the floral pick against the stems so it overlaps about an inch (2-1/2 cm.). Wrap the wire around the stems several times in the same place, and then spiral the wire down the stems. Trim the stems where the wire ends to make perforation easier. The pick can then be wrapped with floral tape if additional strength is needed. Regardless of how you plan to use your floral wire, be sure to have a pair of wire cutters on hand.

### Preserved Materials...

Many fresh evergreens can be picked from the outdoors and then used in a craft project. But if you'd like to pack the project away and use it for next Christmas, you'll need to use glycerin-preserved evergreens.

To glycerin-preserve an evergreen, simply fill a plastic container with three parts water and one part glycerin. Make several angular cuts in the stems of your evergreens and stand them in the liquid for about two weeks. The evergreens will darken slightly in color, and the greenery will become softer and more malleable.

### Glue Guns

Once used only by professionals, glue guns have become an everyday craft tool. They're simple to use: just plug them in, insert a glue stick, and squeeze the trigger. The only complicated part is making sure you don't burn yourself. Besides convenience, the real advantage of a glue gun is that its strong adhesive enables you to glue everything from nuts to wood, and the glue literally dries in seconds.

### Foam

Styrofoam (also known as floral foam, dry foam, or simply foam) can be a crafter's best friend. It's generally inexpensive, and can be bought in any range of shapes from flat to round to tree-shaped. Foam should never show in a finished project.

## Mosses

With the increasing popularity of natural materials, moss has become a common material in many floral projects. Several varieties of mosses are usually available in craft stores, or you can search out your own with the aid of a handbook describing the endangered moss species in your area.

## Ribbon ...

Craft and fabric stores offer a wonderful variety of ribbons in any number of materials, colors, and widths. One of the most exciting craft innovations is the introduction of wired or "French" ribbon to the market. These lovely ribbons, often made from metallic or brocade fabrics, are lined with rows of thin-gauge wire. They do cost more than ordinary ribbon, but the wire allows you to create all kinds of graceful curves.

## Making Wreaths

Begin by choosing a base for your wreath, keeping in mind that your finished wreath will be larger than the base. The most popular bases include foam, vine, straw, and moss bases, although some well-stocked craft stores offer creative alternatives.

Once you've chosen your base, you'll need to decide how to attach your materials. Dried flowers and herbs are often arranged in small bouquets, attached to floral picks, and then inserted into a foam or moss base. The picks are inserted into the base at an angle, and each new pick is positioned to cover the stems of the previous pick. Picks can be used with a vine base by dabbing a small amount of hot glue on the tip of the pick before inserting it into the vines.

Single flower heads, bows, and items such as pinecones or nuts can be hot-glued directly to the base. Heavier items such as seed pods may need to be attached to the base with floral wire first and then secured with hot glue.

## Making Garlands...

Garlands are commonly made by securing short stems of a background material to a base of heavy-gauge wire, raffia, or other material and then hot-gluing accents such as ornaments or special flowers into the background.

First measure cut the base to the length you'd like your finished garland to be. Position several stems of the background material against the base and wrap securely with several loops of spool wire. Position the next group of stems so they cover the previous stems, and again secure with several loops of spool wire. Continue adding the background materials until the base is covered. Add the bow now if one is desired. Last, hot-glue the accent materials in place.

## Making Arrangements...

Begin by preparing a container (a basket, vase, or other interesting vessel) with a block of foam cut to fit. Tape or wire the foam in place and cover the foam with moss using floral pins.

Prepare your materials by adding floral picks to the flowers with weak stems and by cutting the stronger stems at a sharp angle. Insert the flowers into the foam, working to create an oval, round, or triangular outline shape. To add visual interest, place the flowers at varying depths in the foam, placing the darkest colored flowers near the center to draw the eye inward.

## Working with Surface Design...

Years ago, the only place paint went was on paper or canvas, and many of us questioned our ability to paint without numbers. Today the shelves of craft stores are lined with tubes of puff paints, glitter paints, fabric paints, paint pens for wood projects, and opalescent aerosol sprays, just to name a few.

## Fun Paints

If you haven't used puff paints before, you're in for a real treat. Usually sold in small plastic bottles, you simply squeeze the paint onto fabric or other surface. After the paint dries, a few seconds of heat from a steam iron makes the paint puff up — lots of fun. Like puff paints, fabric paints can be used on wood and plastic surfaces, and even on peanuts. (See pages 26 and 27.) Paint pens allow you to create colorful, even outlines on wood and metal surfaces. Enjoy experimenting.

## Acrylic Paints

These permanent paints are to crafters what a box of crayons is to a kid: the more colors you have, the more motivated and creative you feel. Don't let the name "artist's acrylic" on the label scare you. Acrylics are easy to use and clean up easily with water. The color names requested in the materials' lists are universal, so "cadmium red" is "cadmium red", no matter what brand you buy or where you buy it.

Colors can also be mixed to achieve new colors. Mixing the color is fairly simple, but there are a few rules. The fewer colors you mix together, the bet-

ter the brilliance and clarity. When too many colors are mixed together the finished color will be muddy. Always mix substantially less then you think you'll need: you can always mix more if the color is perfect but the paint will be wasted if the color's wrong.

To paint the **poinsettia tray**, the **ark**, or the **Santa fireplace board**, you will need to know a little about shading and highlighting. To simplify the technique, you will need only three values of light, medium, and dark. Always base coat with the medium value and then add your shadows with a darker shade of the same color. Last, add highlights with a lighter, brighter color.

To paint the poinsettia tray, follow the diagram on page 155, keeping the value system in mind. Materials: Numbers 2, 4, and 6 flat tole brushes, liner brush, 2 shades of green oil paint for the leaves (create the dark value with leaf green, black, and burnt umber; create the medium value with dark green mix and yellow citron; and create the veins with leaf green and yellow citron),

3 shades of oil paint for the red leaves (create the dark medium with cadmium red scarlet, carmine, and burnt sienna; create the medium value with dark red mix and cadmium red pale; create the light value with burnt carmine and cadmium red pale; and create the highlight mix with white and cadmium orange), 2 shades of green oil paint for the holly leaves (create the dark value with paynes grey, Prussian blue, and leaf green; create the medium value with dark green mix and more leaf green; and create the highlights with ice blue, yellow citron or white, and a touch of light green), 2 shades of red oil paint for the berries (create the medium value with cadmium red pale and burnt sienna; and create the light value with cadmium red pale).

Instructions for the Tray: Paint a wooden tray with two coats of dark green paint, sanding lightly between coats. Using white graphite paper, trace the poinsettia and holly patterns onto the center and edges of the tray.

Mix small quantities of each color.

Make sure you have enough contrast among the different shades so the leaves will be distinguished from one another. The paint texture should have the consistency of heavy cream.

Green Leaves: Alternate the dark and medium green leaves. Apply dark green to one side of the leaf and medium green to the other. Pat the colors gently and blend them to soften. Wipe (but do not clean) your brush between blending. Do not over blend. Lightly touch in the veins with light green using the liner brush.

Red Leaves: Alternate the shades of red on the leaves so that the bottom leaves are the darkest, using the pattern directions for guidance. Paint the underneath leaves darkest leaves first, using dark and medium red mixes on opposite sides of each leaf. Softly blend the colors together with a wiped brush. Paint the medium and light leaves in the same matter, being sure to use enough contrast between adjacent leaves to separate them. Do the veins in the darkest shade of red with a liner brush.

Flowers: use a #2 brush to apply and blend the colors in the diagram. The base is dark green, yellow citron is in the middle, and red is on top. Brush in hairs with medium and dark reds.

Holly Leaves: Apply medium green mix around the edges of the holly leaves. Fill in the center with the dark green mix and pat gently to blend. Highlight the leaf with white, ice blue, or yellow citron by applying the color next to the darkest green shade. Add the vein with the highlight color.

Holly Berries: Using the liner brush, paint the round berry with the light red mix. Shade in the outer round edge with the medium mix. Dot with burnt sienna for the bottom of the berry and add highlight with a dot of white or yellow for contrast.

After you've finished painting, let the paint dry thoroughly. Clean off any graphite marks and smudges with turpentine and brush on a coat of varnish if you like.

The ark project uses the same three value-system described above. The Santa board is a bit more tricky. If you've been successful with the tray, you're probably ready for the Santa board. Remember to use three shades of each color. The face is flesh; the beard is grey with a white highlight; the suit is red with an orange highlight; the bag, belt, and shoes are brown; and the toys and packages are colors of your choice.

## Paint Washes

To make a wash of color, just add water to your chosen color. The more water you add, the more translucent the color will be. Then brush on a thin layer of the mixture.

## Papier-Mâché

You may remember papier-mâché projects from your school days as messy and unglamorous, but believe us, it's changed. The ornaments and wall hanging on pages 12 and 89 represent just a few of the possibilities. The basic mixture for papier-mâché can be purchased inexpensively in a craft store, and can changed to the color of your choice with just a little paint.

## Modeling Compound

Modeling medium is easy and encouraging to work with. It "fires" in an ordinary kitchen oven in minutes and comes in a variety of colors. You can also create your own colors by mixing several colors of clay together, although you'll want to work with small amounts until you get the color right. Your fired clay projects can also be painted with acrylics if desired.

To complete a project you only need to know the basic techniques of rolling logs, cords, and balls from the clay. Working on a piece of plate glass is helpful because it's smooth and easy to clean. Use the palms of your hands instead of your fingers to roll out the clay and practice until you can achieve uniform shapes.

## Enlarging Patterns...

Although traditional grid paper remains a functional stand-by, the specialized copy machines found in print shops and larger libraries can enlarge patterns to a precise percentage in minutes for a nominal fee. You'll find the percentage of increase marked on the patterns in this book.

# INDEX

●●●●●●

# BIBLIOGRAPHY

●●●●●●●●●●●●●●●●

Allison, Sonia. *The Cassell Food Dictionary*. London, England: Cassell Publishers Limited, 1990.

Bailey, L.H. Hortus Third. New York City, New York: Macmillan Publishing Co., 1976.

Pulleyn, Rob. *The Wreath Book*. New York City, New York: Sterling Publishing Co., 1988.

Pulleyn, Rob and Claudette Mautor. *Everlasting Floral Gifts*. New York City, New York: Sterling Publishing Co., 1989.